PERFORMANCE-BASED EVALUATION FOR CERTIFICATED AND NON-CERTIFICATED SCHOOL PERSONNEL

PERFORMANCE-BASED EVALUATION FOR CERTIFICATED AND NON-CERTIFICATED SCHOOL PERSONNEL

Standards, Criteria, Indicators, Models

Robert D. Buchanan
and
Ruth Ann Roberts

Mellen Studies in Education
Volume 62

The Edwin Mellen Press
Lewiston•Queenston•Lampeter

Library of Congress Cataloging-in-Publication Data

Buchanan, Robert D. (Robert Dewayne)
  Performance-based evaluation for certificated and non-certificated school personnel :
standards, criteria, indicators, models / Robert D. Buchanan, Ruth Ann Roberts.
        p. cm. -- (Mellen studies in education ; v. 62)
  Includes bibliographical references and index.
  ISBN 0-7734-7392-0
  1. School employees--Rating of--United States. 2. School personnel
management--United States. I. Roberts, Ruth Ann. II. Title. III. Series.

  LB2831.58 .B83   2001
  371.2'01--dc21

                                                                    2001016982

This is volume 62 in the continuing series
Mellen Studies in Education
Volume 62 ISBN 0-7734-7392-0
MSE Series ISBN 0-88946-935-0

A CIP catalog record for this book is available from the British Library.

The Edwin Mellen Press   The Edwin Mellen Press
Box 450   Box 67
Lewiston, New York   Queenston, Ontario
USA 14092-0450   CANADA L0S 1L0

The Edwin Mellen Press, Ltd.
Lampeter, Ceredigion, Wales
UNITED KINGDOM SA48 8LT

Printed in the United States of America

DEDICATION

This book is dedicated to public school administrators everywhere who believe the instructional leader's purpose is to support and improve teaching and learning. Only through evaluation and professional development can education be improved.

TABLE OF CONTENTS

The Interstate School Leaders Licensure Consortium (ISLLC), a program of the Council of Chief State School Officers, provided a major advancement for the profession of school administration in its development of the Standard for School Leaders. Future histories of education will surely rank them as a hallmark of late Twentieth-Century American education.

The Standards were drafted by personnel form twenty-four state departments of education and representatives from various professional organizations. The avowed purpose of the Consortium was to "raise the bar for the practice of school leadership." To do this in part, Educational Testing Service was employed to develop certification examinations, which might be used by member states of the consortium in licensing and certification reciprocity.

The exams are in place in Missouri and several other states for the purpose of examining and licensing of building level school leaders. A similar exam for the purpose of examining and licensing school district leaders is presently being utilized in Missouri and will be available in other states in 2001.

Licensing, however, is not the only use the Standards should serve. It is perhaps not even the most important use that may be made of these performance benchmarks. Accountability for performance is a career-long necessity for school leaders and those who employ them. The Standards and their Performance Indicators form a perfect basis to assess the continuing professional work of school administrators and other school personnel as well as provide guidance to professional development. The needs, then, are for evaluative instruments based on the Standards with their Performance Indicators. Professors Buchanan and Roberts have developed and tested such instruments.

Translating the necessarily broad language of the Standards into words of sufficient specificity that evaluators and those being evaluated understand clearly the performance standards as applied to the various professional and non-certificated classifications has been a tedious and lengthy task for the authors. Users of the manual will increasingly appreciate their clarity in developing the various instruments and the performance indicators.

It is hard to overstate the value of their work. This manual is not simply the product of academicians. Both authors are steeped in the real workaday world of the practicing school administrator. Dr. Buchanan served long and well as a secondary school principal and superintendent of schools. Dr. Roberts was also for many years an elementary school administrator and director of the Sikeston schools' elementary education division. They have evaluated many hundreds of school administrators and other employees - certificated and non-certificated. In their capacities, first as adjunct professors and now as full-pledged professors of educational administration, they are immersed in the preparation of new school leaders and all that implies in the way of cutting edge research and study of our great profession. Professors Buchanan and Roberts have contributed handsomely and practically in the development and testing of the materials of this manual. I believe every school administrator will find their manual and the evaluative instruments they provide a perfect means for doing Performance-Based Evaluations of every level of the professional and the non-certificated staff.

Richard F. Farmer, Ph.D., Chairperson Emeritus
Department of Educational Administration & Counseling
Southeast Missouri State University
Cape Girardeau, Missouri 63701

The fundamental role of the administrator or supervisor as an educational leader is that of an evaluator. The method in which an evaluation is conducted and the evaluation results reflect the training, judgment, and expertise of the individuals involved. Major criticisms indicated in past literature pertaining to performance evaluation models have focused on the lack of definition of items used when assessing performance. More importantly, research by the Interstate School Leaders Consortium has established common standards and performances for educational leaders. The standards approach provides the best avenue to allow diverse job roles to be assessed and evaluated. Formal leadership positions in education can share the Interstate School Leaders Consortium Standards for assessment and evaluation. This research not only has proven to be highly practical and valuable for state and national assessments, but it also has provided a strong foundation for the development of a Performance-Based Evaluation model. The *Performance-Based Evaluation Model* was designed for K-12 supervising school administrators and supervisors who wish to help their staffs grow professionally. It clarifies and expands skills the administrator or supervisor will need to use in observing, conferring, and writing evaluations.

Performance-based evaluation is important for all job descriptions in education. Standards provide the expectations and criteria and indicators focus the evaluation of school personnel. School districts may customize criteria and indicators to meet the needs of school improvement initiatives. Both certificated and non-certificated staff profit through the evaluation process, development of performance plans and portfolios. These activities provide reflection time and planning for continued improvement. It is this on-going improvement of each individual that will result in comprehensive school improvement thus providing the ultimate benefit to students.

This manual provides school leaders with templates or models of evaluation tools for various school personnel job descriptions. The models indicate standards, suggested criteria to meet those standards, and suggested indicators of the various criteria. The models can be modified to meet district or building needs and continue to uphold the standards. Practitioners may wish to select different criteria and indicators for each standard to meet the needs of their district. This allows for unique programs and plans that districts wish to implement to be a part of the personnel evaluation tool; thus promoting implementation.

It is recommended that districts utilize teams of personnel to customize the evaluation tools for their districts. It is our intent to assist with a pattern. We believe that professional evaluation requires good tools, good professional training for the evaluators, and open communication with all parties. Those being evaluated should know the standards, criteria, and indicators that are expected and those expectations should promote the vision, mission, and goal accomplishment of the district. Valuable school improvement requires standards (high expectations) for all and that all members of the district be aware of the comprehensive school improvement initiative that the district is striving to implement. We believe the following models will assist school leaders with the development of tools that will assist with the achievement of their desired school improvement goals.

ACKNOWLEDGMENT

We wish to acknowledge Dr. Neil J. Shipman and Dr. Joe Murphy for their permission to reproduce material developed by the Interstate School Leaders Licensure Consortium. Special acknowledgment goes to Dr. Sue Shepard, Chairperson, Department of Educational Administration and Counseling, Southeast Missouri State University.

CHAPTER ONE: PERFORMANCE-BASED ADMINISTRATOR EVALUATION MODEL

THE PURPOSES OF ADMINISTRATOR EVALUATION

THE ROLE OF ISLLC

The Interstate School Leaders Licensure Consortium (ISLLC) has established common standards for school leaders. These standards arise from the struggle to restructure education and the need to redefine the roles of formal school leaders focusing on leadership over management. The Consortium focused on the research that links educational leadership and productive schools, especially regarding student success. A second focus was significant trends in society and education that impact leadership.

ISLLC standards reflect the understanding of the consortium that formal leadership in schools is very complex and multi-faceted. Yet, effective leaders may have different patterns of beliefs and act differently from the norm in the profession. They focus on learning, teaching, and school improvement issues and act as a moral agent and social advocate for students and communities. They lead from a platform that values others as individuals and colleagues within the educational community.

The Consortium identified some powerful societal dynamics, which impact education. The social fabric of society is changing. The pattern of the fabric of society is becoming more diverse racially, linguistically and culturally. Poverty is increasing as are indexes of physical, mental and moral well-being.

The economic foundations of society are being recast as the shift to a post-industrial society, global marketplace, increased reliance on technology, and market-based solutions to social needs provide vectors of force on education. It is these challenges that require new leadership in schools.

When looking to education, ISLLC focused on three central changes all of which demand **a redefined portfolio of leadership skills** for school administrators. One change is a redefinition of learning and teaching to more successfully challenge and engage all youngsters in the education process. Even the views of knowledge, intelligence, assessment and instruction of the past are being renewed. Secondly, community-focused, caring-centered concepts of schooling will compete for legitimacy with the more traditional "institutional" models. Finally, parents, the corporate sector, and community leaders are playing an increasingly significant role in education.

Representatives of the 24 member states and affiliated organizations developed the ISLLC Standards. They delineated standards and indicators which would promote productive leadership, and the standards and indicators were finalized by relying upon the collective wisdom of colleagues in schools and school districts, institutions of higher education, and state or national education groups.

Seven guiding principles focused the efforts of the Consortium and led to the development of six standards. These seven principles were: (ISLLC: Standards for School Leaders, 1996)

- Standards should reflect the centrality of student learning.
- Standards should acknowledge the changing role of the school leader.
- Standards should recognize the collaborative nature of school leadership.
- Standards should be high, upgrading the quality of the profession.
- Standards should inform performance-based systems of assessment and evaluation for school leaders.
- Standards should be integrated and coherent.

- Standards should be predicated on the concepts of access, opportunity, and empowerment for all members of the school community.

These seven principles guided the Consortium to the standards approach. Other education arenas were already using standards for evaluation. The standards approach provides the best avenue to allow diverse job roles to share the standards. All formal leadership positions in education can share the ISLLC Standards and be evaluated based on those standards.

LEGAL REQUIREMENT

Most states require that administrators be evaluated. Missouri public school law RSMO Section 168.410 requires that school administrators and district superintendents be evaluated. The law is as follows:

Evaluation of School Administrators and District Superintendents

School administrators and school district superintendents shall be evaluated in the following manner:

(1) The board of education of each school district shall cause a comprehensive performance-based evaluation for each administrator employed by the district. Such evaluation shall be ongoing and of sufficient specificity and frequency to provide for demonstrated standards of competency and academic ability;

(2) All evaluations shall be maintained in the respective administrator's personnel file at the office of the board of education of the school district. A copy of each evaluation shall be provided to the person being evaluated and to the appropriate administrator;

(3) The state department of elementary and secondary education shall provide suggested procedures for the evaluations performed under this section.

PURPOSE OF ISLLC MODEL

The interstate school leader licensure consortium study to develop standards for school administrators brought some of the best educators and leaders in twenty-six states and together they arrived at consensus regarding six

3

standards. These standards have **knowledge, disposition and performance** components. Each of these component areas has criteria that should be observed if the leader exhibits the standard.

The purpose of this manual is to provide evaluation forms containing the standards, criteria and possible indicators that an evaluator might expect to find exhibited by observation or portfolio documentation. The process of evaluation has two goals. First is the goal of improving leadership and to some degree the management skills of the administrator. Certainly the greater emphasis is on leadership and more importantly, instructional leadership. The second goal is to provide a tool to meet the legal requirements of evaluation.

Formative and summative forms are provided as parallel documents. Each measures all standards and criteria. Every effort has been made to provide opportunities for comment and reflection. **Evaluators cannot be expected to observe administrators exhibit all standards and criteria. Therefore, it is important that the administrator create a record of documentation (professional portfolio) to exhibit to the evaluator.** This record should be considered in observation conferences and become part of the formative process that leads to the development of the summative evaluation.

Professional development and the establishment of goals for personal professional improvement and school improvement are very important. The self-evaluation form provides the opportunity for discussion and the finalization of a professional plan that will benefit the individual and the school or district. A reflection process over the professional year is completed by the administrator and discussed with the supervisor when assessing the professional develop plan accomplishment.

The occasion may arise when a professional improvement plan is necessary. This event can be documented on the professional improvement timeline. The professional improvement form provides an opportunity for the evaluator to express concern and for the administrator being evaluated to develop a plan on a time schedule to show improvement, and establish strategies and

4

activities to accomplish the plan. The reflection process should indicate the administrator's assessment of PIP completion and provide discussion during the conference with the supervisor.

In addition to being aligned with ISLLC, the indicators and professional plans (both leadership and improvement) can and should be aligned with the school improvement plan (SIP). The forms provided are models and any district may modify the process to meet their particular needs.

THE EVALUATION PROCESS MODEL

The process of evaluation is ongoing. However, to focus attention on specific standards and criteria is vital to both individual professional and school improvement issues. The ISLLC standards and criteria are central to such improvement efforts. **Indicators that criteria and standards are exhibited have been listed under the ISLLC criteria on the Performance Based Administrator Evaluation Forms.**

Prior to a scheduled evaluation, the administrator will complete a **Pre-Evaluation Visit Form.** This form is really a plan of what the administrator would like for the evaluator/ supervisor to see during the evaluation session. Since instructional leadership is the goal, the administrator should plan some instructional leadership activities in addition to management activities for the visiting evaluator to observe. This form should be discussed at the pre-observation meeting.

By using a **Formative Performance Based Evaluation Form,** an evaluator and administrator have the opportunity to exhibit and observe a multitude of indicators. The form allows "other" to be selected on every criterion and any indicator which is applicable can be recorded (including artifacts or portfolio items). This form is only one piece of evidence in the evaluation process.

Every administrator will self-evaluate and use the information from the **Self-Evaluation Form** in conjunction with the school improvement plan to develop a **Professional Development Plan** with the evaluator/supervisor. The

PDP should be a year-long effort to improve professionally and assist with the accomplishment of the school improvement plan. The plan could consist of an individual growth plan or a group plan with colleagues. Action research is a possibility or any other plan of action that is mutually acceptable. At the end of the year, reflection on the plan is needed prior to the conference with the evaluator regarding the PDP degree of success.

If an administrator does not meet the district expectation in any area, a **Professional Improvement Plan** must be developed. This plan allows the administrator to know exactly what must be improved and identifies strategies, actions, and a timeline for progress. At the completion of the PIP, reflection should be made prior to conferencing with the supervisor. The plan will be met, not met, or continued as progressing.

To complete the **Summative Evaluation Form**, two formative observations, the PDP and/or PIP, reflections, and portfolio data are utilized. The four indicators from the formative form are carried forward and may be checked to indicate deficiencies or commendables. Documentation form portfolio presentation or other evidence is acceptable and can be noted in comment areas. In the instance that a criterion is checked "below" or "progressing", a professional improvement plan must be developed for each criterion that is not meeting expectation.

As each person reflects on the professional school year, much professional growth can be attained and new plans made for the next year. The **Reflection Form** covers many aspects of the formalized evaluation process and is considered to be a valuable exercise in improvement.

ISLLC STANDARDS AND CRITERIA

The Interstate Leaders Licensure Consortium developed six standards for school leaders. Each standard is focused on learning and teaching as well as the creation of powerful learning environments. Each standard has numerous indicators defined. The indicators are clustered into three areas:

- **Knowledge** (knowledge and understanding)
- **Dispositions** (beliefs, values and commitment)
- **Performances** (facilitates processes and engages in activities)

STANDARD 1 A school administrator is an educational leader who promotes the success of all students by **facilitating the development, articulation, implementation, and stewardship of a vision of learning that is shared and supported by the school community.**

Knowledge

The administrator has knowledge and understanding of:

- ➢ Learning goals in a pluralistic society
- ➢ The principles of developing and implementing strategic plans
- ➢ Systems theory
- ➢ Information sources, data collection, and data analysis strategies
- ➢ Effective communication
- ➢ Effective consensus-building and negotiations skills

Dispositions

The administrator believes in, values, and is committed to:

- ➢ The administrator believes in, values, and is committed to:
- ➢ The educability of all
- ➢ A school vision of high standards of learning
- ➢ Continuous school improvement
- ➢ The inclusion of all members of the school community
- ➢ Ensuring that students have the knowledge, skills, and values needed to become successful adults

7

- A willingness to continuously examine one's own assumptions, beliefs, and practices
- Doing the work required for high levels of personal and organization performance.

Performances

The administrator facilitates processes and engages in activities ensuring that:

- The administrator facilitates processes and engages in activities ensuring that:
- The vision and mission of the school are effectively communicated to staff, parents, students and community members
- The vision and mission are communicated through the use of symbols, ceremonies, stories, and similar activities
- The core beliefs of the school vision are modeled for all stakeholders
- The vision is developed with and among stakeholders
- The contributions of school community members to the realization of the vision are recognized and celebrated
- Progress toward the vision and mission is communicated to all stakeholders
- The school community is involved in school improvement efforts
- The vision shapes the educational programs, plans, and activities
- The vision shapes the educational programs, plans, and actions
- An implementation plan is developed in which objectives and strategies to achieve the vision and goals are clearly articulated
- Assessment data related to student learning are used to develop the school vision and goals
- Relevant demographic data pertaining to students and their families are used in developing the school mission and goals
- Barriers to achieving the vision are identified, clarified, and addressed
- Needed resources are sought and obtained to support the implementation of the school mission and goals

8

- ➢ Existing resources are used in support of the school vision and goals
- ➢ The vision, mission, and implementation plans are regularly monitored, evaluated, and revised

STANDARD 2 A school administrator is an educational leader who promotes the success of all students by **advocating, nurturing, and sustaining a school culture and instructional program conducive to student learning and staff professional growth.**

Knowledge

The administrator has knowledge and understanding of:

- ➢ Student growth and development
- ➢ Applied learning theories
- ➢ Applied motivational theories
- ➢ Curriculum design, implementation, evaluation, and refinement
- ➢ Principles of effective instruction
- ➢ Measurement, evaluation, and assessment strategies
- ➢ Diversity and its meaning for educational programs
- ➢ Adult learning and professional development models
- ➢ The change process for systems, organizations, and individuals
- ➢ The role of technology in promoting student learning and professional growth
- ➢ School cultures

Dispositions

The administrator believes in, values, and is committed to:

- ➢ Student learning as the fundamental purpose of schooling
- ➢ The proposition that all students can learn
- ➢ The variety of ways in which students can learn
- ➢ Life long learning for self and others
- ➢ Professional development as an integral part of school improvement
- ➢ The benefits that diversity brings to the school community

- ➤ A safe and supportive learning environment
- ➤ Preparing students to be contributing members of society

Performances

The administrator facilitates processes and engages in activities ensuring that:

- ➤ All individuals are treated with fairness, dignity and respect
- ➤ Professional development promotes a focus on student learning consistent with the school vision and goals
- ➤ Students and staff feel valued and important
- ➤ The responsibilities and contributions of each individual are acknowledged
- ➤ Barriers to student learning are identified, clarified, and addressed
- ➤ Diversity is considered in developing learning experiences
- ➤ Life long learning is encouraged and modeled
- ➤ There is a culture of high expectations for self, student, and staff performance
- ➤ Technologies are used in teaching and learning
- ➤ Student and staff accomplishments are recognized and celebrated
- ➤ Multiple opportunities to learn are available to all students
- ➤ The school is organized and aligned for success
- ➤ Curricular, co-curricular and extra-curricular programs are designed, implemented, evaluated, and refined
- ➤ Curriculum decisions are based on research, expertise of teachers, and the recommendations of learned societies
- ➤ The school culture and climate are assessed on a regular basis
- ➤ A variety of sources of information regarding performance are used by staff and students
- ➤ Pupil personnel programs are developed to meet the needs of students and their families

STANDARD 3   A school administrator is an educational leader who promotes the success of all students by **ensuring management of the organization, operations, and resources for a safe, efficient and effective learning environment.**

Knowledge

The administrator has knowledge and understanding of:

- ➢ Theories and models of organizations and the principles of organizational development
- ➢ Operational procedures at the school and district level
- ➢ Principles and issues relating to school safety and security
- ➢ Human resources management and development
- ➢ Principles and issues relating to fiscal operations of school management
- ➢ Principles and issues relating to school facilities and use of space
- ➢ Legal issues impacting school operations
- ➢ Current technologies that support management functions

Dispositions

The administrator believes in, values, and is committed to:

- ➢ Making management decisions to enhance learning and teaching
- ➢ Taking risks to improve schools
- ➢ Trusting people and their judgments
- ➢ Accepting responsibility
- ➢ High-quality standards, expectations and performances
- ➢ Involving stakeholders in management processes
- ➢ A save environment

Performances

The administrator facilitates processes and engages in activities insuring that:

- ➢ Knowledge of learning, teaching and student development is used to inform management decisions

- Operational procedures are designed and managed to maximize opportunities for successful learning
- Emerging trends are recognized, studied and applied as appropriate
- Operational plans and procedures to achieve the vision and goals of the school are in place
- Collective bargaining and other contractual agreements related to the school are effectively managed
- The school plant, equipment and support systems operate safely, efficiently and effectively
- Time is managed to maximize attainment of organizational goals
- Potential problems and opportunities are identified
- Problems are confronted and resolved in a timely manner
- Financial, human and material resources are aligned to the goals of schools
- The school acts entrepreneurally to support continuous improvement
- Organizational systems are regularly monitored and modified as needed
- Stakeholders are involved in decisions affecting schools
- Responsibility is shared to maximize ownership and accountability
- Effective problem-framing and problem-solving skills are used
- Effective conflict resolution skills are used
- Effective group-process and consensus building skills are used
- Effective communication skills are used
- There is effective use of technology to manage school operations
- Fiscal resources of the school are managed responsibly, efficiently and effectively
- A safe, clean and aesthetically pleasing school environment is created and maintained
- Human resource functions support the attainment of school goals
- Confidentiality and privacy of school records are maintained

STANDARD 4   A school administrator is an educational leader who promotes the success of all students by **collaborating with families and community members, responding to diverse community interests and needs, and mobilizing community resources.**

Knowledge

The administrator has knowledge and understanding of:

➢ Emerging issues and trends that potentially impact the school community

➢ The conditions and dynamics of the diverse school community

➢ Community resources

➢ Community relations and marketing strategies and processes

➢ Successful models of school, family, business, community, government and higher education partnerships

Dispositions

The administrator believes in, values, and is committed to:

➢ Schools operating as an integral part of the larger community

➢ Collaboration and communication with families

➢ Involvement of families and other stakeholders in school decision-making processes

➢ The proposition that diversity enriches the school

➢ Families as partners in the education of their children

➢ The proposition that families have the best interests of their children in mind

➢ Resources of the family and community needing to be brought to bear on the education of students

➢ An informed public

Performances

The administrator facilitates processes and engages in activities ensuring that:

➢ High visibility, active involvement, and communication with the larger community is a priority

- ➢ Relationships with community leaders are identified and nurtured
- ➢ Information about family and community concerns, expectations, and needs is used regularly
- ➢ There is outreach to different business, religious, political, and service agencies and organizations
- ➢ Credence is given to individuals and groups whose values and opinions may conflict
- ➢ The school and community serve one another as resources
- ➢ Available community resources are secured to help the school solve problems and achieve goals
- ➢ Partnerships are established with area businesses, institutions of higher education, and community groups to strengthen programs and support school goals
- ➢ Community youth family services are integrated with school programs
- ➢ Community stakeholders are treated equitably
- ➢ Diversity is recognized and valued
- ➢ Effective media relations are developed and maintained
- ➢ A comprehensive program of community relations is established
- ➢ Public resources and funds are used appropriately and wisely
- ➢ Community collaboration is modeled for staff
- ➢ Opportunities for staff to develop collaborative skills are provided

STANDARD 5   A school administrator is an educational leader who promotes the success of all students by **acting with integrity, fairness, and in an ethical manner.**

Knowledge

The administrator has knowledge and understanding of:

- ➢ The purpose of education and the role of leadership in modern society
- ➢ Various ethical frameworks and perspectives on ethics
- ➢ The values of the diverse school community
- ➢ Professional codes of ethics

- ➤ The philosophy and history of education

Dispositions

The administrator believes in, values, and is committed to:

- ➤ The ideal of the common good
- ➤ The principles of the Bill of Rights
- ➤ The right of every student to a free, quality education
- ➤ Bringing ethical principles to the decision-making process
- ➤ Subordinating one's own interest to the good of the school community
- ➤ Accepting the consequences for upholding one's principles and actions
- ➤ Using the influence of one's office constructively and productively in the service of all students and their families
- ➤ Development of a caring school community

Performances

The administrator:

- ➤ Examines personal and professional values
- ➤ Demonstrates a personal and professional code of ethics
- ➤ Demonstrates values, beliefs, and attitudes that inspire others to higher levels of performance
- ➤ Serves as a role model
- ➤ Accepts responsibility for school operations
- ➤ Considers the impact of one's administrative practices on others
- ➤ Uses the influence of the office to enhance the educational program rather than for personal gain
- ➤ Treats people fairly, equitable, and with dignity and respect
- ➤ Protects the rights and confidentiality of students and staff
- ➤ Demonstrates appreciation for and sensibility to the diversity in the school community
- ➤ Recognizes and respects the legitimate authority of others
- ➤ Examines and considers the prevailing values of the diverse school community

> Expects that others in the school community will demonstrate integrity and exercise ethical behavior
> Opens the school to public scrutiny
> Fulfills legal and contractual obligations
> Applies laws and procedures fairly, wisely, and considerately

STANDARD 6   A school administrator is an educational leader who promotes the success of all students by **understanding, responding to, and influencing the larger political, social, economic, legal, and cultural context.**

Knowledge

The administrator has knowledge and understanding of:

> Principles of representative governance that undergird the system of American schools
> The role of public education in developing and renewing a democratic society and an economically productive nation
> The laws as related to education and schooling
> The political, social, cultural and economic systems and processes that impact schools
> Models and strategies of change and conflict resolution as applied to the larger political, social, cultural and economic contexts of schooling
> Global issues and forces affecting teaching and learning
> The dynamics of policy development and advocacy under our democratic political system
> The importance of diversity and equity in a democratic society

Dispositions

The administrator believes in, values, and is committed to:

> Education as a key to opportunity and social mobility
> Recognizing a variety of ideas, values, and cultures
> Importance of a continuing dialogue with other decision makers affecting education

16

- Actively participating in the political and policy-making context in the service of education
- Using legal systems to protect student rights and improve student opportunities

Performances

The administrator facilitates processes and engages in activities ensuring that:

- The environment in which schools operate is influenced on behalf of students and their families
- Communication occurs among the school community concerning trends, issues, and potential changes in the environment in which schools operate
- There is ongoing dialogue with representatives of diverse community groups
- The school community works within the framework of policies, laws, and regulations enacted by local, state, and federal authorities
- Public police is shaped to provide quality education for students
- Lines of communication are developed with decision makers outside the school community

PERFORMANCE-BASED ADMINISTRATOR EVALUATION

FORMATIVE REPORT

STANDARD 1   A school administrator is an educational leader who promotes the success of all students by **facilitating the development, articulation, implementation and stewardship of a vision of learning that is shared and supported by the school community.**

The focus of standard one is the ability of the candidate to analyze important aspects of his/her school or district in terms of their impact on student learning. What would you identify as the most significant features of the community in which your school or district exists? How do these features affect student learning? How do these features shape your decision-making and your activities as a school leader? Some of the features that affect student learning could be the demographics of the district, historical, and cultural information, assessment and census date, descriptions of economic factors, or trends.

*Evidence that an administrator meets Standard One is provided by documentation of the following **Knowledge, Disposition and Performance criteria**. Indicators are listed under each criterion with opportunity for additional evidence to be added. Evidence should be provided in the **administrator's portfolio** for the evaluator to use in addition to direct observation of educational leadership.*

Knowledge

The administrator has knowledge and understanding of:

    A. Learning goals in a pluralistic society

        1. ☐   Considers community and school culture in goal development

        2. ☐   Ensures curriculum for a pluralistic society

        3. ☐   Ensures goals for school improvement consider needs of community

        4. ☐   Other _____

    B. The principles of developing and implementing strategic plans

        1. ☐   Develop / implement comprehensive school improvement plan

        2. ☐   Develop / implement plans for improvement of student performance

        3. ☐   Develop / implement plans for academic and support programs

        4. ☐   Other _____

    C. Systems theory

        1. ☐   Demonstrates systems theory in program evaluation

2. ☐ Demonstrates knowledge in budget development / management

3. ☐ Demonstrates in school improvement planning / processes

4. ☐ Other _____

D. Information sources, data collection, and data analysis strategies

1. ☐ Collects and analyzes information from appropriate sources to provide information for the school / district improvement plan(s)

2. ☐ Keeps appropriate required records and use them to improve the school / district

3. ☐ Uses data to assist with the development of the mission and goals that provide the vision of learning for the district

4. ☐ Other _____

E. Effective communication

1. ☐ Demonstrates effective communication skills with fellow educators, students and parents

2. ☐ Demonstrates proficiency in community and media communication

3. ☐ Demonstrates effective communication skills using technology available within the district

4. ☐ Other _____

F. Effective consensus-building and negotiations skills

1. ☐ Effectively builds teams (committees, task forces) to serve the building / district

2. ☐ Leads teams to support district school improvement plans, promote student achievement, and promote a safe, quality, learning environment

3. ☐ Demonstrates the ability to stand firm or compromise appropriately

4. ☐ Other _____

Dispositions

The administrator believes in, values, and is committed to:

    A. The educability of all

        1. ☐   Shows commitment to all students in the school / district

        2. ☐   Assists with program development and evaluation in all facets of the district ensuring appropriate programs for all students

        3. ☐   Supports the learning process for all students by ensuring appropriate schedules, budgets, programs, and support structure

        4. ☐   Other _____

    B. A school vision of high standards of learning

        1. ☐   Demonstrates high expectations for students and staff

        2. ☐   Encourages that policies supporting the school vision and high standards be developed and adopted

        3. ☐   Plans school / district procedures that require all members of the school community to attain high standards

        4. ☐   Other _____

    C. Continuous school improvement

        1. ☐   Improvement plans are continuous with periodic (at least annual) analysis of feedback to determine effectiveness and course of action

        2. ☐   Ensures that all members of the district team participate in professional, support, and program development to improve the performance of all

        3. ☐   Ensures that longitudinal information is maintained to develop an annual district report card or comprehensive report on building / district status

        4. ☐   Other _____

    D. The inclusion of all members of the school community

1. ☐ Promotes the inclusion of business and community members on school committees that are advisory and/or planning for district improvement

2. ☐ Encourages the inclusion of non-school persons in the education process as volunteers, presenters and models of a variety of careers

3. ☐ Works with community groups and service organizations to promote school and community partnerships to benefit all

4. ☐ Other _____

E. Ensuring that students have the knowledge, skills, and values needed to be successful adults

1. ☐ Actively examines curriculum to ensure proper scope and sequence of instruction and age appropriateness or prerequisite requirement

2. ☐ Encourages and assists teaching staff with the development of professional plans that focus on effective instruction and the building / district improvement goals

3. ☐ Uses numerous sources of data to assess student progress toward their chosen pathway of study or preparation for the next grade level or course

4. ☐ Other _____

F. A willingness to continuously examine one's own assumptions, beliefs, and practices

1. ☐ Exhibits desire to improve school practices to benefit the learning climate

2. ☐ Challenges the status quo and the belief systems of all to ensure reflection on values, beliefs, assumptions and the platform from which mission, goals, and the vision of the district was developed

3. ☐ Seeks feedback regarding the assumptions and beliefs of the district and the community to ensure they are harmonious

4. ☐ Other _____

G. Doing the work required for high levels of personal and organization performance.

    1. ☐ Timely meets required deadlines and produces accurate products

    2. ☐ Ensures that the efforts of all are focused toward realization of the school improvement plan

    3. ☐ Exhibits willingness to do whatever it takes to accomplish tasks that are necessary for the daily operation of the school and success of students

    4. ☐ Other _____

Performances

The administrator facilitates processes and engages in activities ensuring that:

A. The vision and mission of the school are effectively communicated to staff, parents, students and community members

    1. ☐ Communication to community patrons regarding the vision and mission of the school is meaningful and frequent.

    2. ☐ Staff members are made to feel important and integral to the accomplishment of the school vision and mission.

    3. ☐ The importance of student success is communicated to the students, teachers and parents as the core component of the vision and mission of the school.

    4. ☐ Other _____

B. The vision and mission are communicated through the use of symbols, ceremonies, stories, and similar activities

    1. ☐ Traditions of the school and district are utilized to further the vision and mission of the school.

2. ☐ A variety of ceremonies and activities are encouraged and supported as methods of vision and mission accomplishment

3. ☐ The community is invited to share in the symbols, ceremonies, and activities that support vision and mission accomplishment

4. ☐ Other _____

C. The core beliefs of the school vision are modeled for all stakeholders

1. ☐ Core beliefs are modeled for all stakeholders through out the building and district (mottos, banners, student work, etc.)

2. ☐ The development of the vision includes all stakeholders including community members (district and/or school improvement committees)

3. ☐ Stakeholder contributions are recognized as important contributions to the realization of the vision, and progress toward reaching the vision is shared with all stakeholders

4. ☐ Other _____

D. The vision is developed with and among stakeholders

1. ☐ Committees of stakeholders work to consider internal factors in need of improvement or attention

2. ☐ Committees of stakeholders work to examine external factors of school

3. ☐ The administrator used information from all stakeholders to develop the mission

4. ☐ Other _____

E. The contributions of school community members to the realization of the vision are recognized and celebrated

1. ☐ Plans for community involvement in vision realization are made

23

2. ☐   There is a sharing of efforts regarding vision attainment

3. ☐   Awards and honors are planned to celebrate community contributions

4. ☐   Other _____

F. Progress toward the vision and mission is communicated to all stakeholders

    1. ☐   Assessment of progress toward vision accomplishment is maintained

    2. ☐   The status of vision attainment is communicated to stakeholders

    3. ☐   Teams and work groups evaluate the progress and adjust plans as needed

    4. ☐   Other _____

G. The school community is involved in school improvement efforts

    1. ☐   The school improvement planning includes representation from the certificated as well as the non-certificated staff in all areas of schooling

    2. ☐   All members of the school community are expected to participate and provide evidence to show their efforts in the school improvement plans

    3. ☐   School improvement is reported to all stakeholders as feedback information for the renewal of school improvement planning

    4. ☐   Other _____

H. The vision shapes the educational programs, plans, and activities

    1. ☐   The district/school vision is used to develop and provide educational programs of the district/school.

    2. ☐   Activities and actions of the district/school are developed to promote the vision.

    3. ☐   Progress toward attaining the vision is assessed annually

4. ☐   Other _____

I.   The vision shapes the educational programs, plans, and actions

    1. ☐   The vision is used in the development of the school improvement plans

    2. ☐   Plans for instructional improvement emanate from the vision

    3. ☐   Activities of the school are organized to bring the vision to fruition

    4. ☐   Other _____

J.   An implementation plan is developed in which objectives and strategies to achieve the vision and goals are clearly articulated.

    1. ☐   A comprehensive implementation plan is developed with input from all sectors of the school community

    2. ☐   The implementation plan for school improvement delineates objectives and strategies to achieve those objectives, responsible parties, and timeline for accomplishment

    3. ☐   The vision, mission, and goals of the district/school are clearly the foundation for the improvement plan.

    4. ☐   Other _____

K.   Assessment data related to student learning are used to develop the school vision and goals

    1. ☐   Assessment data regarding student learning are the basis of the school improvement plan

    2. ☐   Annual analysis and longitudinal data regarding student achievement is used to renew the vision and goals of the district/school

    3. ☐   Demographic data pertaining to students and their families are used during the development of the school mission and goals

25

4. ☐ Other _____

L. Relevant demographic data pertaining to students and their families are used in developing the school mission and goals

    1. ☐ Student demographic data is analyzed for instructional success comparison

    2. ☐ Community and family demographics are used to develop school goals

    3. ☐ The mission and goals are established to meet the needs of varying demographic factors

    4. ☐ Other _____

M. Barriers to achieving the vision are identified, clarified, and addressed

    1. ☐ Progress toward reaching the vision is determined by the annual assessment of the school improvement plan

    2. ☐ Concerns are identified and analyzed to determine cause of lacking progress

    3. ☐ All members of the team are expected to take ownership and assist in the removal of barriers to the achievement of the vision.

    4. ☐ Other _____

N. Needed resources are sought and obtained to support the implementation of the school mission and goals

    1. ☐ The budgeting process focuses on the district/school mission and goals when resources are allocated

    2. ☐ Additional resources are sought as needed to promote the accomplishment of the school improvement plan

    3. ☐ All facets of the school community are expected to support the accomplishment to the school improvement plan with resources such as time, effort, innovative ways to doing things, etc.

    4. ☐ Other _____

26

O. Existing resources are used in support of the school vision and goals

    1. ☐   Budget requests indicate use of resources for vision accomplishment

    2. ☐   Building and scheduling resources focus on goal and vision attainment

    3. ☐   Personnel resources are utilized to accomplish goals and vision

    4. ☐   Other _____

P. The vision, mission, and implementation plans are regularly monitored, evaluated, and revised

    1. ☐   The school improvement plan is monitored annually as set forth in the plan

    2. ☐   Progress reports of the district clearly establish the accomplishments made long and short range

    3. ☐   Barriers or concerns are identified, evaluated and removed or altered to become a positive part of the school improvement plan.

    4. ☐   Other _____

Evaluator Comments   Administrator Comments

_____   _____

_____   _____

_____   _____

STANDARD 2   A school administrator is an educational leader who promotes the success of all students by **advocating, nurturing, and sustaining a school culture and instructional program conducive to student learning and staff professional growth.**

The focus of standard two is the candidate's support of the professional growth and development of staff members directed toward the improvement

of student learning. What are some of the collaborative processes that you would utilize to assist in the establish goals for a specific staff member(s) in your school district? Explain how these goals would be related to student learning. Some information that could be utilized could be notes from meetings with staff members, classroom observation notes, curriculum, instruction, assessment information, journal entries, and relevant letters from parents, students, school improvement plan, etc.

*Evidence that an administrator meets Standard Two is provided by documentation of the following **Knowledge, Disposition and Performance criteria**. Indicators are listed under each criterion with opportunity for additional evidence to be added. Evidence should be provided in the **administrator's portfolio** for the evaluator to use in addition to direct observation of educational leadership.*

Knowledge

The administrator has knowledge and understanding of:

    A. Student growth and development

        1. ☐ Age appropriate standards for students are established

        2. ☐ Curriculum appropriate to the students is provided

        3. ☐ Instructional methods and additional student activities (clubs, sports, etc.) are appropriate to the students of the building

        4. ☐ Other _____

    B. Applied learning theories

        1. ☐ Current and successful learning theories are a major component of professional development for instructional staff.

        2. ☐ Support is provided for staff members who wish to try new instructional methods to improve learning

        3. ☐ Successful learning theories are shared among staff during grade level or departmental meetings

        4. ☐ Other _____

C. Applied motivational theories

    1. ☐   Current and successful motivational theories are a major component of professional development for instructional staff.

    2. ☐   Support is provided for staff members who wish to try new motivational methods to improve learning

    3. ☐   Successful motivational strategies are shared among staff during grade level or departmental meetings

    4. ☐   Other _____

D. Curriculum design, implementation, evaluation, and refinement

    1. ☐   Designing the curriculum is a major focus of the district/school

    2. ☐   Lesson plan review, classroom visits, departmental and/or grade level meetings, and individual discussions ensure curriculum implementation

    3. ☐   The degree of student success (including disaggregated data) is utilized to evaluate and refine the curriculum

    4. ☐   Other _____

E. Principles of effective instruction

    1. ☐   Current and successful instructional strategies are a major component of professional development for instructional staff.

    2. ☐   Support is provided for staff members who wish to try new instructional methods to improve learning

    3. ☐   Successful instructional strategies are shared among staff during grade level or departmental meetings

    4. ☐   Other _____

F. Measurement, evaluation, and assessment strategies

1. ☐ Attention is given to the proper measurement of student success, goal attainment, school improvement success, and vision accomplishment
2. ☐ The entire school improvement plan is given attention when evaluating the success of the process of education
3. ☐ A variety of assessment strategies are expected with particular attention being given to performance tasks and constructed responses.
4. ☐ Other _____

G. Diversity and its meaning for educational programs
   1. ☐ Diversity of the school is taken into account when developing programs
   2. ☐ Curriculum that is positive to minority students is a part of the instructional program
   3. ☐ Diverse student groups are included in the total school activities
   4. ☐ Other _____

H. Adult learning and professional development models
   1. ☐ All staff members are expected to participate in training to improve skills
   2. ☐ Professional development is planned within the school and district
   3. ☐ To maximize professional growth, staff members have professional development plans with instructional goals
   4. ☐ Other _____

I. The change process for systems, organizations, and individuals
   1. ☐ Renewal is the spirit of change, keeping what is good and making it better
   2. ☐ System and organizational renewal is a part of the district/school improvement plan

3. ☐ Individuals are expected to participate in reflection and renewal of their instructional processes

4. ☐ Other _____

J. The role of technology in promoting student learning and professional growth

1. ☐ The use of technology in the daily curriculum is a prime consideration

2. ☐ Staff members are expected to be proficient in the use of technology for all aspects of the educational process

3. ☐ Students are coached regarding the use of technology as tools of learning and expected to regularly use technology within the curriculum

4. ☐ Other _____

K. School cultures

1. ☐ School cultures are respected

2. ☐ Diversity of culture is used to benefit the student educational process

3. ☐ Staff members are encouraged to promote student acceptance of diversity

4. ☐ Other

Dispositions

The administrator believes in, values, and is committed to:

A. Student learning as the fundamental purpose of schooling

1. ☐ Focus support functions of the district/school on student learning.

2. ☐ Fiscal support of the school improvement plan centers on student learning

3. ☐ Curriculum and instruction is assessed and renewed to promote improved student learning

4. ☐ Other _____

B. The proposition that all students can learn

    1. ☐   High expectations exist for all students including the successful completion of individual education plans

    2. ☐   Curriculum and instruction allows for assessment of student success and the remediation or challenge as needed

    3. ☐   Students are encouraged to select a program of studies that will allow them to successfully progress to further education or a job

    4. ☐   Other _____

C. The variety of ways in which students can learn

    1. ☐   Staff members are expected to be able to identify various learning styles of students and use this knowledge in selection of teaching strategies

    2. ☐   Attention to active participation and authentic learning is stressed

    3. ☐   Professional development in current instructional practices is stressed for all teachers

    4. ☐   Other _____

D. Life long learning for self and others

    1. ☐   Professional development plans for staff members continue the learning process for instructional staff

    2. ☐   The instructional team is encouraged to share the successful experiences among themselves

    3. ☐   Administrator stays current regarding trends for instruction, team building, and student learning

    4. ☐   Other _____

E. Professional development as an integral part of school improvement

    1. ☐   School improvement plans include ample professional development aimed at improvement of instruction

2. ☐ Administrative professional development regarding team building, inclusion of the community, public relations and student data analysis

3. ☐ Networking within and among buildings focuses on the sharing of positive, successful techniques to improve student learning

4. ☐ Other _____

F. The benefits that diversity brings to the school community

1. ☐ Diversity is celebrated as reality of the world

2. ☐ Cultural variety is promoted as a strength of the school and community

3. ☐ Opportunities are provided for the school and community to share cultural and ethnic celebrations

4. ☐ Other _____

G. A safe and supportive learning environment

1. ☐ Facilities and transportation are inspected regularly to ensure a safe school

2. ☐ Continual efforts are made to support the learning efforts of all students

3. ☐ Procedures are developed for the safe and efficient daily running of the school in a manner that supports student learning

4. ☐ Other _____

H. Preparing students to be contributing members of society

1. ☐ Instructional efforts include application to community and society

2. ☐ Plans of study for senior high students include curriculum that prepares students to enter post-secondary training/college or become employed

3. ☐   Opportunities for students to participate in class and community projects to ensure the understanding of their role in a democratic society

4. ☐   Other _____

Performances

The administrator facilitates processes and engages in activities ensuring that:

A. All individuals are treated with fairness, dignity and respect

    1. ☐   Policies and procedures engender fairness to all

    2. ☐   Dignity and respect are held in high esteem by faculty and administration and are modeled for students

    3. ☐   School personnel, parents and students are all respected for their importance and contributions for the community of learners

    4. ☐   Other _____

B. Professional development promotes a focus on student learning consistent with the school vision and goals

    1. ☐   School improvement plans include ample professional development aimed at improvement of instruction

    2. ☐   Administrative professional development regarding team building, inclusion of the community, public relations and student data analysis to ensure attainment of vision and goals of the school/district

    3. ☐   Networking within and among buildings focuses on the sharing of positive, successful techniques to improve student learning

    4. ☐   Other _____

C. Students and staff feel valued and important

    1. ☐   Interaction with students both inside and outside the classroom makes them realize that they are important members of the school community

2. ☐ Instructional staff members are empowered to be partners in the learning environment of the school/district

3. ☐ Support staff members are valued and their importance to the learning process is verbalized and celebrated within the school community

4. ☐ Other _____

D. The responsibilities and contributions of each individual are acknowledged

1. ☐ Ceremonies and traditions are established to reward and honor staff and students who are responsible contributors to the learning community

2. ☐ Contributions are praised through school and community news outlets as well as school award traditions

3. ☐ Student extra-curricular clubs and activities that engender Responsibilities are available for student participation

4. ☐ Other _____

E. Barriers to student learning are identified, clarified, and addressed

1. ☐ The examination and evaluation of student data is utilized to identify barriers or concerns regarding student learning

2. ☐ All who are involved in the student learning process are included in the identification and clarification of student learning problems

3. ☐ School improvement plans are developed to identify strategies and actions necessary to achieve improved student learning

4. ☐ Other _____

F. Diversity is considered in developing learning experiences

1. ☐ Staff professional development assists with the planning of learning experiences that use diversity to benefit the learning of all

35

2. ☐ Sharing of diversity within the school is promoted by administration

3. ☐ Opportunities for the celebration of diversity are provided

4. ☐ Other _____

G. Life long learning is encouraged and modeled

1. ☐ Opportunities for professional development are provided and utilized by the building and district level administration

2. ☐ Modeling of involvement in new education endeavors is provided by the administration for the instructional staff

3. ☐ Students are encouraged to develop the skills of life long learners

4. ☐ Other _____

H. There is a culture of high expectations for self, student, and staff performance

1. ☐ The administrator establishes and demonstrates high expectations for his/her role in the process of student learning

2. ☐ Expectations for staff performance at an exemplary level are established and communicated to the staff

3. ☐ A climate promoting student performance at the highest levels is established by the administrator

4. ☐ Other _____

I. Technologies are used in teaching and learning

1. ☐ The use of technology in the daily curriculum is a prime consideration

2. ☐ Staff members are expected to be proficient in the use of technology for all aspects of the educational process

3. ☐ Students are coached regarding the use of technology as tools of learning and expected to regularly use technology within the curriculum

4. ☐ Other _____

J. Student and staff accomplishments are recognized and celebrated

    1. ☐ The school/district ensures that student accomplishments in academics, extra-curricular activities, and other endeavors are honored and that the successes are communicated to the public

    2. ☐ Staff accomplishments are recognized by the administration and encouraged to further student learning

    3. ☐ Communication of outstanding efforts by staff and students to the press and other news media as well as student publications is ongoing

    4. ☐ Other _____

K. Multiple opportunities to learn are available to all students

    1. ☐ As an instructional leader, the administrator coaches teaching staff to provide more than one opportunity for each student to learn

    2. ☐ Professional development opportunities concerning learning styles and teaching strategies are deemed important and included in the district/school program selection

    3. ☐ Teachers are encouraged to include a variety of strategies in their classroom instruction

    4. ☐ Other _____

L. The school is organized and aligned for success

    1. ☐ Processes for smooth daily operation of the school are established and reviewed periodically to ensure an orderly environment

    2. ☐ The success of each student and the student population as a whole is always the visible goal of the entire school/district

3. ☐ Communication of the importance of a safe and orderly environment that is aligned for success is continual within and outside the building/district

4. ☐ Other _____

M. Curricular, co-curricular and extra-curricular programs are designed, implemented, evaluated, and refined

1. ☐ Considerable attention is given to the design and implementation of the curriculum into the instructional program daily.

2. ☐ Data from a variety of sources is analyzed to determine the effectiveness of the curriculum and instruction of the district and refinement occurs where needed.

3. ☐ Co- and extra-curricular programs are expected to meet the needs of students and consistent evaluation and refinement is accomplished to keep the programs responsive to student needs.

4. ☐ Other _____

N. Curriculum decisions are based on research, expertise of teachers, and the recommendations of learned societies

1. ☐ Administrative and teaching staff members are expected to maintain an awareness and understanding of current research findings regarding curriculum and student learning

2. ☐ Teachers are expected to assume ownership of the curriculum and instruction process as well as efforts to improve the process of learning

3. ☐ Input is expected from recognized organizations that are outstanding in the curriculum and instruction processes

4. ☐ Other _____

O. The school culture and climate are assessed on a regular basis

1. ☐ The administrator uses multiple sources of information from within the school regarding the culture and climate of the school

2. ☐ Analysis of community input is an important component in the determination of positive school culture and climate

3. ☐ Every effort is made to ensure that the school culture and climate is integral to the positive learning environment

4. ☐ Other _____

P. A variety of sources of information regarding performance are used by staff and students

1. ☐ Evaluation of student learning is based on different sources of information including products as well as examinations

2. ☐ Standardized testing is used in student and program evaluation

3. ☐ Staff and students are included in the evaluation of performance as the reflect on the learning environment and expected performance tasks

4. ☐ Other _____

Q. Pupil personnel programs are developed to meet the needs of students and their families

1. ☐ Students and their parents are encouraged to meet with the school counselor regarding the academic program and the possible courses of study that a student could choose

2. ☐ Parents are expected to meet with the teacher(s) that a student has to develop plans for the school year and establish rapport

3. ☐ Dialog is on going between the school and the home to provide the needed support for students, parents and teachers

4. ☐ Other _____

_____   _____

_____   _____

_____   _____

STANDARD 3   A school administrator is an educational leader who
promotes the success of all students by **ensuring
management of the organization, operations, and
resources for a safe, efficient and effective learning
environment.**
**The focus of standard three is the candidate's advancement of student
learning through the resolution of competing claims by two or more
individuals or parties regarding the allocation of resources, staff, and time
within his/her school or district.** What are some of the opposing groups, or
factions who have competing claims over the allocation of resources? What are
the potential educational impacts of allocating the resources unfairly? What are
some of the areas of competing claims besides resources that an administrator
must manage?

_Evidence that an administrator meets Standard Three is provided by
documentation of the following **Knowledge, Disposition and Performance
criteria**. Indicators are listed under each criterion with opportunity for additional
evidence to be added. Evidence should be provided in the **administrator's
portfolio** for the evaluator to use in addition to direct observation of educational
leadership._

<u>Knowledge</u>

The administrator has knowledge and understanding of:

    A. Theories and models of organizations and the principles of
organizational development

        1. ☐   The administrator used theories and models of
organizations as he/she organizes the school/district

40

2. ☐ Principles of organizational development are used to provide an organization that is responsive to internal and external forces

3. ☐ The administrator can effectively maneuver among the theories as needed

4. ☐ Other _____

B. Operational procedures at the school and district level

1. ☐ Procedures for daily operation of the school / district are understood by all

2. ☐ An environment conducive to learning is a prime consideration in development of the operational procedures

3. ☐ Record keeping processes document operational procedures

4. ☐ Other _____

C. Principles and issues relating to school safety and security

1. ☐ Safety procedures are known to all and practiced regularly

2. ☐ Emergency management plans are in place and updated regularly

3. ☐ Strict adherence to the visitor policy is maintained at all times

4. ☐ Other _____

D. Human resources management and development

1. ☐ Policies are in place to guide certificated and non-certificated personnel

2. ☐ Grievance policies are in place to assist with settling disagreements

3. ☐ Attention is given to professional and work skill development for all

4. ☐ Other _____

E. Principles and issues relating to fiscal operations of school management

41

1. ☐ Budget planning provides for the maximization of learning
2. ☐ Curricular as well as extra-curricular programs are supported fiscally
3. ☐ Proper records are kept when dealing with fiscal matters
4. ☐ Other _____

F. Principles and issues relating to school facilities and use of space

1. ☐ Facilities are maintained to promote the learning atmosphere
2. ☐ Facilities are utilized completely to support student learning and activities
3. ☐ Appropriate improvement planning is accomplished annually
4. ☐ Other _____

G. Legal issues impacting school operations

1. ☐ Current legislation is assessed regarding school / district impact
2. ☐ Court rulings that impact schools are considered and shared with others
3. ☐ The administrator is knowledgeable of compliance issues
4. ☐ Other _____

H. Current technologies that support management functions

1. ☐ Exhibits proficiency in use of technologies that support management
2. ☐ Programs and equipment are updated
3. ☐ Student records are maintained confidentially in databases
4. ☐ Other _____

Dispositions

The administrator believes in, values, and is committed to:

A. Making management decisions to enhance learning and teaching

1. ☐ Management procedures support the learning process

2. ☐ Management decisions focus on teaching and learning processes
3. ☐ Facilitates the success of students
4. ☐ Other _____

B. Taking risks to improve schools
  1. ☐ Exhibits willingness to pilot new projects
  2. ☐ Evaluates and initiates change when it is appropriate
  3. ☐ Empower staff members to make decisions and try new things
  4. ☐ Other _____

C. Trusting people and their judgments
  1. ☐ Is able to delegate and willing to accept the judgments of others
  2. ☐ Solicits feedback following evaluation of programs and/or practices
  3. ☐ Considers the administrative team as trustworthy
  4. ☐ Other _____

D. Accepting responsibility
  1. ☐ Assumes the responsibility for all decisions regarding the school
  2. ☐ Is responsible for fiscal, managerial, and leadership events and processes
  3. ☐ Makes decisions based on policy, procedure, and what is best for students
  4. ☐ Other _____

E. High-quality standards, expectations and performances
  1. ☐ Exhibits high expectations and standards for administration and staff
  2. ☐ Communicated high standards and expectations of students

43

3. ☐   Includes parents in partnerships for high performance expectations for students

4. ☐   Other _____

F. Involving stakeholders in management processes

     1. ☐   Students and staff are involved in development of school processes

     2. ☐   Parents and community are included in advisory efforts

     3. ☐   Volunteers/community members are invited to participate in the process of schooling

     4. ☐   Other _____

G. A save environment

     1. ☐   Drills and practices are held on a regular basis

     2. ☐   Codes and proactive processes are reviewed with staff regularly

     3. ☐   Proper safety codes and expectations are met

     4. ☐   Other_____

Performances

The administrator facilitates processes and engages in activities insuring that:

A. Knowledge of learning, teaching and student development is used to inform management decisions

     1. ☐   Makes management decisions based on improving student learning

     2. ☐   Facilitates improvement of instruction through management

     3. ☐   Considers student development and interest when making decisions

     4. ☐   Other _____

B. Operational procedures are designed and managed to maximize opportunities for successful learning

1. ☐ District/school procedures for daily operation focus on student learning

2. ☐ Management of school/district activities and procedures considers the benefit and welfare of the learner

3. ☐ Student and faculty input is utilized to develop management decisions

4. ☐ Other _____

C. Emerging trends are recognized, studied and applied as appropriate

   1. ☐ The administrator keeps up with current trends in education

   2. ☐ Time is spent sharing new ideas and determining whether or not adoption would improve instruction within the district/school

   3. ☐ Staff members are encouraged to follow the model of the administrator and consider new trends in education that would be appropriate

   4. ☐ Other _____

D. Operational plans and procedures to achieve the vision and goals of the school are in place

   1. ☐ The district / school improvement plan is in place and supports the vision

   2. ☐ The administrator brings the focus of the plans and procedures back to the school and district improvement plans

   3. ☐ The administrator is a team player, ensuring that all school plans support the district comprehensive improvement plan

   4. ☐ Other _____

E. Collective bargaining and other contractual agreements related to the school are effectively managed

   1. ☐ The administrator works with faculty to ensure effective instruction

2. ☐ The administrator upholds the contractual agreements of the district

3. ☐ The administrator assumes his/her appointed role within district policy

4. ☐ Other _____

F. The school plant, equipment and support systems operate safely, efficiently and effectively

1. ☐ Regular checks of school plant equipment regarding proper operation and safety are made

2. ☐ Interaction with support personnel ensures safe and efficient operation

3. ☐ All support is focused on creating an effective learning environment

4. ☐ Other _____

G. Time is managed to maximize attainment of organizational goals

1. ☐ Efficient time management techniques are practiced by the administrator

2. ☐ Learning time is protected

3. ☐ Good skills are practiced when organizing and leading meetings

4. ☐ Other _____

H. Potential problems and opportunities are identified

1. ☐ The administrator practices good observation techniques

2. ☐ The administrator is proactive in problem solving

3. ☐ Opportunities to improve the school and staff are maximized

4. ☐ Other _____

I. Problems are confronted and resolved in a timely manner

1. ☐ The administrator is available and approachable

2. ☐ When possible, problems are evaluated carefully

3. ☐ Problems are resolved in a timely manner with student success in mind

4. ☐ Other _____

J. Financial, human and material resources are aligned to the goals of schools

   1. ☐ The district budget is focused on success of the school improvement plan

   2. ☐ District personnel are utilized in ways to maximize expertise and learning

   3. ☐ Learning resources are procured to enhance goal accomplishment

   4. ☐ Other _____

K. The school acts entrepreneurially to support continuous improvement

   1. ☐ Attention is given to support of school improvement entrepreneurially

   2. ☐ Partnerships are developed with community members and businesses

   3. ☐ Schedules ongoing upgrade of school procedures, programs, and facilities

   4. ☐ Other _____

L. Organizational systems are regularly monitored and modified as needed

   1. ☐ Curricular and instructional systems are regularly monitored and modified

   2. ☐ Operating procedures and processes are upgraded as needed

   3. ☐ Information is routinely gathered regarding the progress and success of the system

   4. ☐ Other _____

M. Stakeholders are involved in decisions affecting schools

1. ☐ Efforts are made to include community, parents, students, and faculty in the gathering of district / school information
2. ☐ Representatives of all stakeholder groups are included in committee examination and advisory groups
3. ☐ Efforts are made to ensure that the community supports the school
4. ☐ Other _____

N. Responsibility is shared to maximize ownership and accountability
   1. ☐ All members of the certificated and non-certificated staff are expected to share the responsibility for learning
   2. ☐ Administrator and the school team share responsibility for student success
   3. ☐ Students are aware of the expectations and responsibility for learning
   4. ☐ Other _____

O. Effective problem-framing and problem-solving skills are used
   1. ☐ Administrator effectively evaluates the parameters and effects of problems
   2. ☐ Administrator includes proper stakeholders when problem solving
   3. ☐ Problems are solved in a thorough and timely manner
   4. ☐ Other _____

P. Effective conflict resolution skills are used
   1. ☐ Stakeholders are included in the resolution of problems
   2. ☐ Communication skills to clarify the conflict are evidenced by clear communication of all sides of the conflict
   3. ☐ The solution or resolution is clearly understood by all involved
   4. ☐ Other _____

Q. Effective group-process and consensus building skills are used

1. ☐ The administrator exhibits effective group leadership skills
2. ☐ Consensus building occurs regularly in school / district management
3. ☐ Professional leadership to accomplish the vision and improvement of the school / district is exhibited
4. ☐ Other _____

R. Effective communication skills are used
1. ☐ Listening skills are exhibited by the administrator
2. ☐ The administrator uses clear language understood by all parties and correct grammar
3. ☐ Communication is appropriate to the audience and may be written or verbal
4. ☐ Other _____

S. There is effective use of technology to manage school operations
1. ☐ Student information is managed through the use of technology
2. ☐ Technology is used whenever appropriate in executing job responsibilities
3. ☐ Record keeping and documentation are accomplished with technology
4. ☐ Other _____

T. Fiscal resources of the school are managed responsibly, efficiently and effectively
1. ☐ Proper record keeping ensures fiscal responsibility
2. ☐ Fiscal allocations are managed to promote the learning process of students
3. ☐ Care of equipment and supplies, good inventory technique, and plans for future need are evidenced
4. ☐ Other _____

U. A safe, clean and aesthetically pleasing school environment is created and maintained

    1. ☐   Attention is given to the cleanliness and safety of the school / district

    2. ☐   Resources are allocated for attention to the aesthetic appeal of the school / district

    3. ☐   The school and community are involved in the maintenance of a safe, clean, and proper learning environment

    4. ☐   Other _____

V. Human resource functions support the attainment of school goals

    1. ☐   Personnel resources are allocated to the attainment of the school improvement plan

    2. ☐   Both certificated and non-certificated personnel are expected to complete their responsibilities regarding school district improvement

    3. ☐   Collegiality among personnel promotes the accomplishment of school goals

    4. ☐   Other _____

W. Confidentiality and privacy of school records are maintained

    1. ☐   All student information is shared only with parents and those legally allowed to have the information

    2. ☐   Employee records are confidentially managed by the administrator

    3. ☐   Updates on confidentiality are provided to district employees annually

    4. ☐   Other _____

Evaluator Comments   Administrator Comments

_____   _____

_____   _____

_____   _____

Standard 4   A school administrator is an educational leader who promotes the success of all students by **collaborating with families and community members, responding to diverse community interests and needs, and mobilizing community resources.**

The focus of standard four is the candidate's collaboration with families and the community in order to advance student learning. Describe one partnership that you, either individually or as part of a team, have developed between your school/district and area businesses, institutions of higher education, and/or other community groups and leaders that had a significant impact on student learning in your school or district.   Explain and evaluate the specific impacts that this partnership had on student learning.

*Evidence that an administrator meets Standard Four is provided by documentation of the following **Knowledge, Disposition and Performance criteria**. Indicators are listed under each criterion with opportunity for additional evidence to be added.   Evidence should be provided in the **administrator's portfolio** for the evaluator to use in addition to direct observation of educational leadership.*

Knowledge

The administrator has knowledge and understanding of:

    A. Issues and trends that impact the school community.

        1. ☐   Understands community political dynamics

        2. ☐   Knows what stakeholders can contribute

        3. ☐   Understands the decision-making processes

        4. ☐   Other _____

    B. The conditions and dynamics of the diverse school community.

        1. ☐   Knowledge of the socio-economic conditions of the community

        2. ☐   Involves minority citizens in the school community

3. ☐ School committees reflect the demographics of the community

4. ☐ Other _____

C. Community Resources.

   1. ☐ Utilizes parents, citizens, and community leaders on school committees.

   2. ☐ Ensures communication with local and state social agencies.

   3. ☐ Develops a partnership with local businesses and corporations.

   4. ☐ Other _____

D. Community relations and marketing strategies and processes.

   1. ☐ Understands the value of public relations for the school

   2. ☐ Ensures that an on-going public relations program is provided

   3. ☐ A variety of public relations strategies are utilized

   4. ☐ Other _____

E. Successful models of school, family, business, community, government and higher education partnerships.

   1. ☐ Develops school-business partnerships

   2. ☐ Recruits government agencies to promote the success of the school

   3. ☐ Involves higher education in professional development programs

   4. ☐ Other _____

Dispositions

The administrator believes in, values, and is committed to:

A. Schools operating as an integral part of the larger community.

   1. ☐ Supports the school's involvement in community activities

   2. ☐ Encourages the community to utilize school facilities

3. ☐   Encourages students and staff participation in school and community events

4. ☐   Other _____

B. Collaboration and communication with families.

1. ☐   Cooperates with stakeholders to promote the success of students

2. ☐   Involves staff to communicate successes of students and school

3. ☐   Utilizes a variety of methods to communicate with stakeholders

4. ☐   Other _____

C. Involvement of families and other stakeholders in school decision-ma processes.

1. ☐   Values involvement of stakeholders in school programs and decisions

2. ☐   Actively recruits stakeholders for advisory committees

3. ☐   Provides information to stakeholders to promote informed decision making

4. ☐   Other _____

D. The proposition that diversity enriches the school.

1. ☐   Ensures the representation of all socio-economic groups in the

2. ☐   Policies and procedures of the school promote diversity

3. ☐   Considers culture of stakeholders in curriculum decisions

4. ☐   Other _____

E. Families as partners in the education of their children.

1. ☐   Solicits involvement of parents in developing student's academic plan

2. ☐   Jointly communicates expectation for success of student

3. ☐   Considers culture and socio-economic factors of families in decision making

53

4. ☐   Other _____

F. Resources of the family and community needing to be brought to bear on 1 education of student

     1. ☐   Ensuring that local resources are sufficient to meet the needs of the school

     2. ☐   Ensuring that state resources are sufficient to meet the needs of the school

     3. ☐   Ensuring that Federal resources are sufficient to meet the needs of the school

     4. ☐   Other _____

G. An informed public.

     1. ☐   Develops programs to keep the public informed

     2. ☐   Utilizes available local media to inform public of school events and issues

     3. ☐   Utilizes staff and community members to assist in disseminating information

     4. ☐   Other _____

Performances

The administrator facilitates processes and engages in activities ensuring that:

A. High visibility, active involvement, and communication with the larger community are a priority?

     1. ☐   Actively participates in civic organizations

     2. ☐   Visibly active in the social functions of the community

     3. ☐   Promotes the successes of the community

     4. ☐   Other _____

B. Relationships with community leaders are identified and nurtured.

     1. ☐   Assist community leaders to promote community projects

     2. ☐   Makes available school resources for community projects

     3. ☐   Recognizes community members for assisting the school and students

4. ☐   Other _____

C. Information about family and community concerns, expectations, and needs is used regularly.

    1. ☐   Community demographic information is utilized to make decisions

    2. ☐   Current research information is utilized in the decision-making process

    3. ☐   Advisory committees are recruited to communicate the community's expectations

    4. ☐   Other _____

D. There is outreach to different business, religious, political, and service agencies and organizations.

    1. ☐   School-Business partnerships are developed

    2. ☐   Meetings with the Ministerial Alliance is frequent and on-going

    3. ☐   Local government and service agencies are solicited to provide assistance

    4. ☐   Other _____

E. Credence is given to individuals and groups whose values and opinions may conflict.

    1. ☐   School Committees reflect the diversity of the population community

    2. ☐   Regular meeting are scheduled for the stakeholders to provide comments

    3. ☐   policies and procedures are communicated to provide for conflicting opinions

    4. ☐   Other _____

F. The school and community serve one another as resources.

    1. ☐   School facilities, equipment, and staff are available for community utilization

55

2. ☐ Policies and procedures are revised as needed to promote community utilization

3. ☐ Community facilities and personnel are utilized where appropriate

4. ☐ Other _____

G. Partnerships are established with area businesses, institutions of higher education, and community groups to strengthen programs and support school goals.

1. ☐ School-business partnerships are developed

2. ☐ Professional development programs are developed colleges/universities

3. ☐ Civic and booster organizations are recruited

4. ☐ Other _____

H. Community youth family services are integrated with school programs.

1. ☐ The school disseminates information regarding youth programs

2. ☐ A community/school calendar is jointly developed

3. ☐ School and community facilities are utilized

4. ☐ Other _____

I. Community stakeholders are treated equitably.

1. ☐ Efforts are made to employ staff that reflects the demographics of the community

2. ☐ Policies and procedures are reviewed to ensure that all stakeholders are treated equability

3. ☐ Representation on school committees reflect the demographics of the community

4. ☐ Other _____

J. Effective media relations are developed and maintained.

1. ☐ Background information for programs and events is provided when requested
2. ☐ Information requested by the news media will be provided in a timely manner
3. ☐ Accommodations for parking, seating, and note taking are provided for the news media
4. ☐ Other _____

K. A comprehensive program of community relations is established.
1. ☐ A community and school calendar is developed jointly and disseminated to the community
2. ☐ The school and community will jointly promote the community as a place to live and work
3. ☐ Monthly newsletters will be distributed to stakeholders by the school
4. ☐ Other _____

L. Public resources and funds are used appropriately and wisely.
1. ☐ Annual audits will be conducted and information reported to stakeholders
2. ☐ Policies/procedures exist to ensure expenditures comply with legal requirements
3. ☐ Requests for information regarding school financial data are provided upon request
4. ☐ Other _____

M. Community collaboration is modeled for staff.
1. ☐ Volunteer's personal time and resources
2. ☐ Promotes community projects to school personnel
3. ☐ Active participation in community organizations is evident
4. ☐ Other _____

N. Opportunities for staff to develop collaborative skills are provided.

1. ☐ Staff members are encouraged to participate in community events during the school day

2. ☐ Staff members are nominated for district, state, and national appointments

3. ☐ Financial support and release time will be provided when needed

4. ☐ Other _____

Evaluator Comments   Administrator Comments

_____   _____

_____   _____

_____   _____

STANDARD 5   A school administrator is an educational leader who promotes the success of all students by **acting with integrity, fairness, and in an ethical manner.**

The focus of standard five is the understanding that the candidate has of the value of the diverse school community. The candidate is committed to using the influence of one's office constructively and productively in the service of all students and families. The administrator must examine and consider the prevailing values of the diverse school community. He/she treats people fairly, equitably, and with dignity and respect. He/she demonstrates values, beliefs, and attitudes that inspire others to higher levels of performance.

*Evidence that an administrator meets Standard Five is provided by documentation of the following **Knowledge, Disposition and Performance criteria**. Indicators are listed under each criterion with opportunity for additional evidence to be added. Evidence should be provided in the **administrator's portfolio** for the evaluator to use in addition to direct observation of educational leadership.*

<u>Knowledge</u>

The administrator has knowledge and understanding of:

    A. The purpose of education and the role of leadership in modern society.

58

1. ☐ Ensures participation of all students in the educational process
2. ☐ Demonstrates knowledge of leadership methods
3. ☐ Remains current on new issues and programs in education
4. ☐ Other _____

B. Various ethical frameworks and perspectives on ethics.
1. ☐ Is ethical in dealing with privileged information
2. ☐ Observes the confidentiality of students and their families
3. ☐ Demonstrates the belief that all stakeholders are treated fairly
4. ☐ Other _____

C. The values of the diverse school community.
1. ☐ Mutual respect between stakeholders is evident
2. ☐ Is sensitive to all beliefs and views of various groups in the community
3. ☐ Demonstrates knowledge of student interest, ability, and home background
4. ☐ Other _____

D. Professional codes of ethics.
1. ☐ Demonstrates knowledge of board of education policy pertaining to ethics
2. ☐ Demonstrates knowledge of professional organizations standards on ethics
3. ☐ Demonstrates behavior that reflect a code of ethics
4. ☐ Other _____

E. The philosophy and history of education.
1. ☐ Demonstrates a knowledge of the philosophy of education
2. ☐ Demonstrates a knowledge of the history of education
3. ☐ Implements programs that reflect the philosophy and history of education

59

4. ☐ Other _____

Dispositions

The administrator believes in, values and is committed to:

    A. The ideal of the common good.

        1. ☐ Believes that public education exist for all students

        2. ☐ Believes that schools exist for the teaching and learning of students

        3. ☐ Shows commitment to all students

        4. ☐ Other _____

    B. The principles in the Bill of Rights.

        1. ☐ Supports / implement the legal requirements for public education

        2. ☐ Supports / implement the belief that students have the right to a free public education

        3. ☐ Supports / demonstrates the teaching of democracy in school / district

        4. ☐ Other _____

    C. Bringing ethical principles to the decision-making process.

        1. ☐ Demonstrates a knowledge of the ethical standards of the profession

        2. ☐ Understands personal convictions and their ethical implication

        3. ☐ Understands the rights and responsibilities of members of the school community

        4. ☐ Other _____

    D. Subordinating one's own interest to the good of the school community.

        1. ☐ Accepts and reacts to constructive criticism objectively and professionally

        2. ☐ Adheres to official policies and procedures

        3. ☐ Is supportive of school and community

4. ☐   Other _____

E. Accepting the consequences for upholding one's principles and actions.

    1. ☐   Proceeds in a rational, self-controlled, mature manner

    2. ☐   Evaluates actions and review impact on school / district

    3. ☐   Respects the opinions of other

    4. ☐   Other _____

F. Using the influence of one's office constructively and productively in the service of all students and their families.

    1. ☐   Demonstrates a belief that the school / district exist for the education of the students

    2. ☐   Believes the school / district gives priority to the welfare of the students

    3. ☐   Uses office to promote the value of education for students in the community

    4. ☐   Other _____

G. Development of a caring school community.

    1. ☐   Emphasizes personal and professional standards of integrity

    2. ☐   Supports the belief that ethics should guide what we do in schools

    3. ☐   Understands and respects different cultural standards and beliefs

    4. ☐   Other _____

Performances

The administrator:

A. Examines personal and professional values.

    1. ☐   Develops with the school community to establish expectation for ethical conduct

    2. ☐   Models good ethical judgment

    3. ☐   Reacts to unethical behavior

4. ☐   Other _____

B. Demonstrates a personal and professional code of ethics.

    1. ☐   Understands the ethical standards of the profession

    2. ☐   Models good ethical judgment

    3. ☐   Accepts responsibility for his/her actions

    4. ☐   Other _____

C. Demonstrates values, beliefs, and attitudes that inspire others to higher levels of performance.

    1. ☐   Develops programs to recognize and celebrate academic success

    2. ☐   Implements programs to motive and model on going learning

    3. ☐   Supports the professional development of others

    4. ☐   Other _____

D. Serves as a role model.

    1. ☐   Models the importance of life-long learning

    2. ☐   Understands the literature on teaching and learning

    3. ☐   Supports the need for the school community to appreciate diversity

    4. ☐   Other _____

E. Accepts responsibility for school operations.

    1. ☐   Implements procedures to comply with local, state, and federal regulations

    2. ☐   Develops / assesses the effectiveness of management practices and procedures

    3. ☐   Ensures that community resources are used appropriately

    4. ☐   Other _____

F. Considers the impact of one's administrative practices on others.

    1. ☐   Monitor / evaluate the effectiveness of school programs

2. ☐ Implements modifications to school programs where necessary

3. ☐ Solicits the opinions and concerns of others

4. ☐ Other _____

G. Uses the influence of the office to enhance the educational program rather than for personal gain.

1. ☐ Makes decisions with impartiality, honesty, compassion, and empathy

2. ☐ Works with the school community to establish expectations for ethical conduct

3. ☐ Demonstrates good ethical judgment

4. ☐ Other _____

H. Treats people fairly, equitably, and with dignity and respect

1. ☐ Demonstrates sensitivity to the feelings of others

2. ☐ Addresses unethical behavior

3. ☐ Ensures that policies and procedures are fairly implemented

4. ☐ Other _____

I. Protects the rights and confidentiality of students and staff

1. ☐ Ensures that student and staff information is secured properly

2. ☐ Addresses situations where confidential information is improperly used

3. ☐ Provides professional development regarding confidentiality (legality)

4. ☐ Other _____

J. Demonstrates appreciation for and sensitivity to the diversity in the school community

1. ☐ Furthers cooperation and teamwork among the school community

2. ☐ Recruits minority students, parents, and citizens to serve on committees

3. ☐ Involves all segments of the community in policy development

4. ☐ Other _____

K. Opens the school to public scrutiny

   1. ☐ Provides information regarding the operation of the school to the public

   2. ☐ Reviews accuracy and considers possible effects of information that is provided to the public

   3. ☐ Provides information requested by the media and public in a timely manner

   4. ☐ Other _____

L. Fulfills legal and contractual obligations

   1. ☐ Demonstrates compliances with laws and procedures fairly, wisely, and considerately

   2. ☐ Follows district and legal procedures for financial reporting and budgeting

   3. ☐ Requires the staff to use materials and supplies as required by district policies/procedures

   4. ☐ Other _____

Evaluator Comments   Administrator Comments

_____   _____

_____   _____

_____   _____

STANDARD 6   A school administrator is an educational leader who promotes the success of all students by **understanding, responding to, and influencing the larger political, social, economic, legal, and cultural context.**

64

The focus of standard six is the candidate's and his/her staff's response to a larger (a statewide, regional, or national) political, social, economic, legal, or cultural issue/ trend that negatively affects student learning in the candidate's school or district. Identify and describe the what, who, where, and when of the issue/trend that negatively affects student learning. What are some examples of communication from parents, teachers, students, (that both affect students and their peers), student work samples, teacher logs and lesson plans, etc., issue/trend? What could be the impact of this response on student learning?

*Evidence that an administrator meets Standard Six is provided by documentation of the following **Knowledge, Disposition and Performance criteria**. Indicators are listed under each criterion with opportunity for additional evidence to be added. Evidence should be provided in the **administrator's portfolio** for the evaluator to use in addition to direct observation of educational leadership.*

Knowledge

The administrator has knowledge and understanding of:

    A. Principles of representative governance that under gird the system of American schools

        1. ☐   Understands the importance of a democratic society

        2. ☐   Understands the history of public education in America

        3. ☐   Understands the value of local representation in public education

        4. ☐   Other _____

    B. The role of public education in developing and renewing a democratic society and an economically productive nation

        1. ☐   Understands that public education has a responsibility to teach the history of America

        2. ☐   Understands business and education are connected

        3. ☐   Understands that public education must provide training for future leaders and business

        4. ☐   Other _____

C. The law as related to education and schooling
1. ☐　Demonstrates a knowledge of state public school law
2. ☐　Demonstrates a knowledge of federal public school law
3. ☐　Demonstrates a knowledge of court cases that impact public school law
4. ☐　Other _____

D. The political, social, cultural, and economic systems and processes that impact schools
1. ☐　Understands the local financial system that funds public education
2. ☐　Understands the state financial system that funds public education
3. ☐　Understands the federal financial system that funds public education
4. ☐　Other _____

E. Models and strategies of change and conflict resolution as applied to the larger political, social, cultural and economic contexts of schooling
1. ☐　Understands the research on collaboration, empowerment, and school improvement
2. ☐　Understands group processes
3. ☐　Understands the community's political dynamics
4. ☐　Other _____

F. Global issues and forces affecting teaching and learning
1. ☐　Understands the impact of a global economy on public education
2. ☐　Understands that public education is responsible for preparing students for the world of work
3. ☐　Knows what stakeholders can contribute to develop a world-class school
4. ☐　Other _____

G. The dynamics of policy development and advocacy under our democratic political system

    1. ☐   Demonstrates ability to adapt leadership style to fit the needs of the staff, students, and patrons

    2. ☐   Understands the decision-making processes

    3. ☐   Demonstrates sensitivity to feelings of others, and responds accordingly

    4. ☐   Other _____

H. The importance of diversity and equity in a democratic society

    1. ☐   Understands the need for procedures to permit the staff, students, and patrons to review and formulate recommendations for school/unit goals

    2. ☐   Understands that programs must reflect the values of the community

    3. ☐   Understands that the district must work with parent-teachers and other organizations to improve the service that the district renders to students and the community

    4. ☐   Other _____

Dispositions

The administrator believes in, values, and is committed to:

A. Education as a key to opportunity and social mobility

    1. ☐   Believes all children can learn

    2. ☐   Values learning as the number one priority

    3. ☐   Views all experiences as learning opportunities

    4. ☐   Other _____

B. Recognizing a variety of ideas, values, and cultures

    1. ☐   Values the opinions and concerns of others

    2. ☐   Believes people will respect each other's contributions when diversity is appreciated

3. ☐ Understands and respects different cultural standards and beliefs

4. ☐ Other _____

C. Importance of a continuing dialogue with other decision makers affecting education

   1. ☐ Works with the school community to set high standards for learning

   2. ☐ Works with others to develop and communicate plans and procedures for teaching, learning, and student assessment

   3. ☐ Believes parents, the community, and the schools are partners in the educational process

   4. ☐ Other _____

D. Actively participating in the political and policy-making context in the service of education

   1. ☐ Believes that stakeholders should make decisions in the best interest of students

   2. ☐ Believes empowerment and collaboration are essential for school improvement

   3. ☐ Communicates with the public concerning the nature and rationale of various school programs

   4. ☐ Other _____

E. Using legal systems to protect student rights and improve student opportunities

   1. ☐ Coordinates programs with various local, state, and federal agencies

   2. ☐ Coordinates with local police to ensure smooth functioning of school programs

   3. ☐ Organizes community members to lobby for support for students and school programs

   4. ☐ Other _____

Performances

The administrator facilitates processes and engages in activities ensuring that:

A. The environment in which schools operate is influenced on behalf of students and their families

    1. ☐   Works with stakeholders to establish goals and to set priorities for implementing the school's vision

    2. ☐   Works with the school community to set high standards of learning

    3. ☐   Helps develop the shared understanding and values, which lead to a climate of openness, fairness, mutual respect, support, and inquiry

    4. ☐   Other _____

B. Communication occurs among the school community concerning trends, issues, and potential changes in the environment in which schools operate

    1. ☐   Communicates the school's vision, goals, and priorities to appropriate constituencies

    2. ☐   Achieves consensus and facilitates closure

    3. ☐   Involves stakeholders in school planning and decision making

    4. ☐   Other _____

C. There is ongoing dialogue with representatives of diverse community groups

    1. ☐   Works with stakeholders to set school improvement goals and plans for achieving them

    2. ☐   Exercises leadership role in developing mechanisms for integration of various cultural groups in the school

    3. ☐   Organizes community members to lobby for support for programs in which he/she community have a special interest

4. ☐ Other _____

D. The school community works within the framework of policies, laws, and regulations enacted by local, state, and federal authorities

    1. ☐ Monitors the racial/sexual composition of student groups and the compliance of the school with the provisions of Title IX

    2. ☐ Meets with various parties involved (teachers, parents, students, and professional people) in accordance with legal requirements

    3. ☐ Monitors compliance requirements for all programs under his/her supervision

    4. ☐ Other _____

E. Public policy is shaped to provide quality education for students

    1. ☐ Communicates with the public concerning the nature and rationale of various school programs

    2. ☐ Forms collaborative work groups to set challenging goals for school improvement and to develop strategies for achieving those goals

    3. ☐ Involves stakeholders in the development of a broad vision of what the school should be and a plan for how to get there

    4. ☐ Other _____

F. Lines of communication are developed with decision makers outside the school community

    1. ☐ Communicates priorities regarding resources and material to the state legislature and the U.S. Congress

    2. ☐ Establishes communication lines with the social agencies regarding the needs of the students

    3. ☐ Develops communication channels for minorities to voice concerns

    4. ☐ Other _____

Evaluator Comments   Administrator Comments

_____   _____

_____   _____

_____   _____

Signatures indicate the discussion and sharing of information regarding the formative evaluation. Copies will be provided to the administrator and supervisor/evaluator.

_____   _____
Evaluator's Signature   Administrator's Signature
____/_____/_____   ____/_____/_____
Date   Date

PRE EVALUATION VISIT

The Pre-Evaluation Visit form is to be completed by the administrator and discussed with the evaluator/supervisor at the pre-observation conference. The administrator should focus on the inclusion of instructional leadership activities as a part of the scheduled observation.

Administrator_____School_____

Job Role_____Date___/_____/_____/_____

1. Briefly describe the planned leadership events/activities:_____

_____
_____
_____
_____
_____
_____
_____
_____

2. What professional skills do you want the evaluator to see?_____

_____
_____
_____
_____

3. What school improvement tasks will be addressed?_____

_____
_____
_____
_____
_____

4. What specific ISLLC Standards and Criteria do you want to exhibit?_____

_____

_____

_____

_____

_____

_____

SELF EVALUATION FORM

The administrator prior to developing a Professional Development Plan uses the Self-Evaluation Form. This form should be shared with the administrator's supervisor when conferencing for the PDP.

Administrator_____ Date___/____/_____

Professional Development Plan_____

1. What has been the most positive aspect of your administrative position over the last few years._____

   _____

   _____

   _____

   _____

   _____

2. What area of the formative evaluation was the most difficult for you?_____

   _____

   _____

   _____

   _____

3. Which one of the six standards in the Performance Based Administrator Evaluation do you feel you were the most successful in completing this past year? What evidence can you use to show this success?_____

   _____

   _____

   _____

   _____

4. Which standard would you target as an area for you to improve?_____

   _____

   _____

_____

_____

_____

5. If you had last year to do over, what administrative practices would you change?_____

_____

_____

_____

_____

6. What are some of the administrative activities or ideas that you would share with other?_____

_____

_____

_____

_____

7. What would you like to learn more about, whether it is from another administrator, a university program, or other resources?_____

_____

_____

_____

_____

_____

8. In working with teachers, what skills do you possess that allow for positive and productive outcomes?_____

_____

_____

_____

_____

_____

9. What are your strengths as an administrator?_____

_____

_____

_____

_____

_____

10. What areas of your administration would you like to improve?_____

_____

_____

_____

_____

_____

PROFESSIONAL DEVELOPMENT PLAN

☐ *INITIAL CERTIFICATE*

☐ *RENEWAL OF CERTIFICATE*

☐ *ADVANCED CERTIFICATE*

NOTE: As a part of the Professional Development Plan, it is strongly suggested that administrators remain aware of the Initial Certificate, Renewal of Certificate, and Advanced Certificate renewal processes so that requirements for renewal can become part of the Professional Development Plan.

Administrator_____District_____

Building_____

Supervisor_____Date_____/_____/_____

Criteria: (Note: Administrators must meet all of the certification requirements for principals/superintendents and should address those requirements not completed in the Professional Development Plan.)

Related Building/CSIP Goal(s):

Objectives (applicable descriptors):

Strategies for achieving objective(s):
(Administrator and Supervisor responsibilities)

Administrator will:

Supervisor will:

Assessment methods and timelines:

Supervisor/Evaluator Comments: Administrator's Comments:

_____   _____

_____   _____

_____   _____

_____   _____

Plan developed:

_____ Date / /   _____ Date / /

Supervisor's Signature   Administrator's Signature

Plan completed_____   Plan revised_____Plan continued_____

Date plan reviewed_____/____/_____

_____ Date / /   _____ Date / /

Supervisor's Signature   Administrator's Signature

Signatures indicate that the above has been review and discussed. Copies will be provided to the administrator and supervisor.

PROFESSIONAL IMPROVEMENT PLAN

The professional Improvement Plan is used to assist administrators' not meeting district expectations in one or more criteria. *The supervisor can assign a Professional Improvement Plan at any time a deficiency is noted as progressing or below expectations.*

Administrator_____ Date___/___/___ Building_____

Standard(s):

Knowledge/Disposition/Performance Indicator(s):

Activities/ Steps to be Taken	Resources/ Persons Needed	Data to be Collected	Timelines/ Deadlines	Initial Approval

_____ Date /   /   _____ Date /   /

Supervisor/Evaluator's Signature   Administrator's Signature

Plan Completed_____   Plan revised_____   Plan continued_____

Date plan reviewed___/_____/_____

_____ Date /   /   _____ Date /   /

Supervisor/Evaluator's Signature   Administrator's signature

Signatures indicate that the above has been review and discussed. Copies will be provided to the administrator and supervisor.

STANDARD 1 A school administrator is an educational leader who promotes the success of all students by **facilitating the development, articulation, implementation and stewardship of a vision of learning that is shared and supported by the school community.**

*Evidence that an administrator meets Standard One is provided by documentation of the following Knowledge, Disposition and Performance criteria. Indicators are listed under each criterion with opportunity for additional evidence to be added. Evidence should be provided in the administrator's portfolio for the evaluator to use in addition to direct observation of educational leadership. The administrator will be evaluated as <u>exceeds, meets, is progressing or falls below</u> performance standards. A mark of one or two will require that a Performance Improvement Plan be completed. (4 = **exceeds standards**, 3 = **meets standards**, 2 = **progressing** to a level of meeting standards consistently, 1 = **does not meet standards**, and NA = **does not apply**)*

Knowledge

The administrator has knowledge and understanding of:

A. Learning goals in a pluralistic society   4 3 2 1 NA
   Formative Indicator   1 ☐   2 ☐   3 ☐   4 ☐

B. The principles of developing and implementing
   strategic plans   4 3 2 1 NA
   Formative Indicator   1 ☐   2 ☐   3 ☐   4 ☐

C. Systems theory   4 3 2 1 NA
   Formative Indicator   1 ☐   2 ☐   3 ☐   4 ☐

C. Information sources, data collection, and data
   analysis strategies   4 3 2 1 NA
   Formative Indicator   1 ☐   2 ☐   3 ☐   4 ☐

E. Effective communication   4 3 2 1 NA

Formative Indicator 1☐ 2☐ 3☐ 4☐

F. Effective consensus-building and negotiations

skills   4 3 2 1 NA

Formative Indicator 1☐ 2☐ 3☐ 4☐

Dispositions

The administrator believes in, values, and is committed to:

A. The educability of all   4 3 2 1 NA

  Formative Indicator   1☐ 2☐ 3☐ 4☐

B. A school vision of high standards of learning   4 3 2 1 NA

  Formative Indicator   1☐ 2☐ 3☐ 4☐

C. Continuous school improvement   4 3 2 1 NA

  Formative Indicator   1☐ 2☐ 3☐ 4☐

D. The inclusion of all members of the school

community   4 3 2 1 NA

  Formative Indicator   1☐ 2☐ 3☐ 4☐

E. Ensuring that students have the knowledge,

  skills, and values needed to be successful adults 4 3 2 1 NA

  Formative Indicator   1☐ 2☐ 3☐ 4☐

F. A willingness to continuously examine one's

  assumptions, beliefs, and practices   4 3 2 1 NA

  Formative Indicator   1☐ 2☐ 3☐ 4☐

G. Doing the work required for high levels of

  personal and organizational performance.   4 3 2 1 NA

  Formative Indicator   1☐ 2☐ 3☐ 4☐

Performances

The administrator facilitates processes and engages in activities ensuring that:

A. The vision and mission of the school are effectively

  communicated to staff, parents, students and

  community   4 3 2 1 NA

  Formative Indicator   1☐ 2☐ 3☐ 4☐

B. The vision and mission are communicated through the use of symbols, ceremonies, stories, and similar activities   4 3 2 1 NA

Formative Indicator   1 ☐ 2 ☐ 3 ☐ 4 ☐

C. The core beliefs of the school vision are modeled for all stakeholders   4 3 2 1 NA

Formative Indicator   1 ☐ 2 ☐ 3 ☐ 4 ☐

D. The vision is developed with and among Stakeholders   4 3 2 1 NA

Formative Indicator   1 ☐ 2 ☐ 3 ☐ 4 ☐

E. The contributions of school community members to the realization of the vision are recognized and celebrate   4 3 2 1 NA

Formative Indicator   1 ☐ 2 ☐ 3 ☐ 4 ☐

F. Progress toward the vision and mission is communicated to all stakeholders   4 3 2 1 NA

Formative Indicator   1 ☐ 2 ☐ 3 ☐ 4 ☐

G. The school community is involved in school improvement efforts   4 3 2 1 NA

Formative Indicator   1 ☐ 2 ☐ 3 ☐ 4 ☐

H. The vision shapes the educational programs, plans, and activities   4 3 2 1 NA

Formative Indicator   1 ☐ 2 ☐ 3 ☐ 4 ☐

I. The vision shapes the educational programs, plans, and actions   4 3 2 1 NA

Formative Indicator   1 ☐ 2 ☐ 3 ☐ 4 ☐

J. An implementation plan is developed where objectives And strategies to achieve the vision / goals are clearly articulated.   4 3 2 1 NA

Formative Indicator   1 ☐ 2 ☐ 3 ☐ 4 ☐

K. Assessment data related to student learning are used to
develop the school vision and goals   4   3   2   1   NA

Formative Indicator   1 ☐   2 ☐   3 ☐   4 ☐

L. Relevant demographic data pertaining to students and their
families are used in developing the school
mission and goals   4   3   2   1   NA

Formative Indicator   1 ☐   2 ☐   3 ☐   4 ☐

M. Barriers to achieving the vision are identified, clarified,
and addressed   4   3   2   1   NA

Formative Indicator   1 ☐   2 ☐   3 ☐   4 ☐

N. Needed resources are sought and obtained to support the
implementation of the school mission and goals 4   3   2   1   NA

Formative Indicator   1 ☐   2 ☐   3 ☐   4 ☐

O. Existing resources are used in support of the school
vision and goals   4   3   2   1   NA

Formative Indicator   1 ☐   2 ☐   3 ☐   4 ☐

P. The vision, mission, and implementation plans are
regularly monitored, evaluated, and revised   4   3   2   1   NA

Formative Indicator   1 ☐   2 ☐   3 ☐   4 ☐

STANDARD ONE COMMENTS

Evaluator Comments   Administrator Comments

_____   _____

_____   _____

_____   _____

STANDARD 2   A school administrator is an educational leader who promotes the success of all students by **advocating, nurturing, and sustaining a school culture and instructional program conducive to student learning and staff professional growth.**

Evidence that an administrator meets Standard Two is provided by documentation of the following Knowledge, Disposition and Performance criteria. Indicators are listed under each criterion with opportunity for additional evidence to be added. Evidence should be provided in the administrator's portfolio for the evaluator to use in addition to direct observation of educational leadership. The administrator will be evaluated as <u>exceeds, meets, is progressing or falls below</u> performance standards. . A mark of one or two will require that a Performance Improvement Plan be completed. (4 = exceeds standards, 3 = meets standards,
***2 = progressing** to a level of meeting standards consistently, **1 = does not meet standards**, and **NA = does not apply**)*

<u>Knowledge</u>

The administrator has knowledge and understanding of:

A. Student growth and development   4 3 2 1 NA

     Formative Indicator   1☐   2☐   3☐   4☐

B. Applied learning theories   4 3 2 1 NA

     Formative Indicator   1☐   2☐   3☐   4☐

C. Applied motivational theories   4 3 2 1 NA

     Formative Indicator   1☐   2☐   3☐   4☐

D. Curriculum design, implementation, evaluation, and

     refinement   4 3 2 1 NA

     Formative Indicator   1☐   2☐   3☐   4☐

E. Principles of effective instruction   4 3 2 1 NA

     Formative Indicator   1☐   2☐   3☐   4☐

F. Measurement, evaluation, and assessment

     strategies   4 3 2 1 NA

     Formative Indicator   1☐   2☐   3☐   4☐

G. Diversity and its meaning for educational

     programs   4 3 2 1 NA

     Formative Indicator   1☐   2☐   3☐   4☐

H. Adult learning and professional

development models   4 3 2 1 NA

Formative Indicator   1☐ 2☐ 3☐ 4☐

I.   The change process for systems, organizations, and

Individuals   4 3 2 1 NA

Formative Indicator   1☐ 2☐ 3☐ 4☐

J.   The role of technology in promoting student learning and

professional growth   4 3 2 1 NA

Formative Indicator   1☐ 2☐ 3☐ 4☐

K. School cultures   4 3 2 1 NA

Formative Indicator   1☐ 2☐ 3☐ 4☐

Dispositions

The administrator believes in, values, and is committed to:

A.   Student learning as the fundamental purpose

of schooling   4 3 2 1 NA

Formative Indicator   1☐ 2☐ 3☐ 4☐

B.   The proposition that all students can learn   4 3 2 1 NA

Formative Indicator   1☐ 2☐ 3☐ 4☐

C.   The variety of ways in which students

can learn   4 3 2 1 NA

Formative Indicator   1☐ 2☐ 3☐ 4☐

D. Life long learning for self and others   4 3 2 1 NA

Formative Indicator   1☐ 2☐ 3☐ 4☐

E.   Professional development as an integral part of school

improvement   4 3 2 1 NA

Formative Indicator   1☐ 2☐ 3☐ 4☐

F.   The benefits that diversity brings to the school

community   4 3 2 1 NA

Formative Indicator   1☐ 2☐ 3☐ 4☐

G. A safe and supportive learning environment   4 3 2 1 NA

Formative Indicator   1☐ 2☐ 3☐ 4☐

H. Preparing students to be contributing
members of society   4   3   2   1   NA
Formative Indicator   1 ☐   2 ☐   3 ☐   4 ☐

Performances

The administrator facilitates processes and engages in activities ensuring that:

A. All individuals are treated with fairness,
dignity and respect   4   3   2   1   NA
Formative Indicator   1 ☐   2 ☐   3 ☐   4 ☐

B. Professional development promotes a focus on student
learning consistent with the school vision
and goals   4   3   2   1   NA
Formative Indicator   1 ☐   2 ☐   3 ☐   4 ☐

C. Students and staff feel valued and important   4   3   2   1   NA
Formative Indicator   1 ☐   2 ☐   3 ☐   4 ☐

D. The responsibilities and contributions of each individual
are acknowledged   4   3   2   1   NA
Formative Indicator   1 ☐   2 ☐   3 ☐   4 ☐

E. Barriers to student learning are identified, clarified, and
addressed   4   3   2   1   NA
Formative Indicator   1 ☐   2 ☐   3 ☐   4 ☐

F. Diversity is considered in developing
learning experiences   4   3   2   1   NA
Formative Indicator   1 ☐   2 ☐   3 ☐   4 ☐

G. Life long learning is encouraged and modeled   4   3   2   1   NA
Formative Indicator   1 ☐   2 ☐   3 ☐   4 ☐

H. There is a culture of high expectations for self, student,
and staff performance   4   3   2   1   NA
Formative Indicator   1 ☐   2 ☐   3 ☐   4 ☐

I. Technologies are used in teaching and learning   4   3   2   1   NA
Formative Indicator   1 ☐   2 ☐   3 ☐   4 ☐

J. Student and staff accomplishments are recognized and
    celebrated   4 3 2 1 NA
    Formative Indicator   1 ☐   2 ☐   3 ☐   4 ☐

K. Multiple opportunities to learn are available
    to all students   4 3 2 1 NA
    Formative Indicator   1 ☐   2 ☐   3 ☐   4 ☐

L. The school is organized and aligned for
    success   4 3 2 1 NA
    Formative Indicator   1 ☐   2 ☐   3 ☐   4 ☐

M. Curricular, co-curricular and extra-curricular programs are
    designed, implemented, evaluated, and refined   3 2 1 NA
    Formative Indicator   1 ☐   2 ☐   3 ☐   4 ☐

N. Curriculum decisions are based on research, expertise of
    teachers, and the recommendations of learned
    societies   4 3 2 1 NA
    Formative Indicator   1 ☐   2 ☐   3 ☐   4 ☐

O. The school culture and climate are assessed
    on a regular basis   4 3 2 1 NA
    Formative Indicator   1 ☐   2 ☐   3 ☐   4 ☐

P. A variety of sources of information regarding performance
    are used by staff and students   4 3 2 1 NA
    Formative Indicator   1 ☐   2 ☐   3 ☐   4 ☐

Q. Pupil personnel programs are developed to meet the needs
    of students and their families   4 3 2 1 NA
    Formative Indicator   1 ☐   2 ☐   3 ☐   4 ☐

STANDARD TWO COMMENTS

Evaluator Comments   Administrator Comments

_____   _____

_____   _____

_____   _____

STANDARD 3   A school administrator is an educational leader who promotes the success of all students by **ensuring management of the organization, operations, and resources for a safe, efficient and effective learning environment.**

*Evidence that an administrator meets Standard Three is provided by documentation of the following Knowledge, Disposition and Performance criteria. Indicators are listed under each criterion with opportunity for additional evidence to be added. Evidence should be provided in the administrator's portfolio for the evaluator to use in addition to direct observation of educational leadership. The administrator will be evaluated as <u>exceeds, meets, is progressing or falls below</u> performance standards. A mark of one or two will require that a Performance Improvement Plan be completed. (4 = **exceeds standards**, 3 = **meets standards**, 2 = **progressing** to a level of meeting standards consistently, 1 = **does not meet standards**, and NA = does not apply)*

Knowledge

The administrator has knowledge and understanding of:

A. Theories and models of organizations and the principles
of organizational development   4 3 2 1 NA
    Formative Indicator   1 ☐   2 ☐   3 ☐   4 ☐

B. Operational procedures at the school and
district level   4 3 2 1 NA
    Formative Indicator   1 ☐   2 ☐   3 ☐   4 ☐

C. Principles and issues relating to school
safety and security   4 3 2 1 NA
    Formative Indicator   1 ☐   2 ☐   3 ☐   4 ☐

D. Human resources management and
development   4 3 2 1 NA
    Formative Indicator   1 ☐   2 ☐   3 ☐   4 ☐

E. Principles and issues relating to fiscal operations of school

90

management   4 3 2 1 NA

Formative Indicator 1☐ 2☐ 3☐ 4☐

F. Principles and issues relating to school facilities and

 use of space   4 3 2 1 NA

 Formative Indicator 1☐ 2☐ 3☐ 4☐

G. Legal issues impacting school operations 4 3 2 1 NA

 Formative Indicator 1☐ 2☐ 3☐ 4☐

H. Current technologies that support management

 functions   4 3 2 1 NA

  Formative Indicator 1☐ 2☐ 3☐ 4☐

Dispositions

The administrator believes in, values, and is committed to:

A. Making management decisions to enhance learning

 and teaching   4 3 2 1 NA

 Formative Indicator 1☐ 2☐ 3☐ 4☐

B. Taking risks to improve schools   4 3 2 1 NA

 Formative Indicator 1☐ 2☐ 3☐ 4☐

C. Trusting people and their judgments 4 3 2 1 NA

 Formative Indicator 1☐ 2☐ 3☐ 4☐

D. Accepting responsibility   4 3 2 1 NA

 Formative Indicator 1☐ 2☐ 3☐ 4☐

E. High-quality standards, expectations and

 performances   4 3 2 1 NA

 Formative Indicator 1☐ 2☐ 3☐ 4☐

F. Involving stakeholders in management processes 4 3 2 1

 NA

 Formative Indicator 1☐ 2☐ 3☐ 4☐

G. A safe environment   4 3 2 1 NA

 Formative Indicator 1☐ 2☐ 3☐ 4☐

Performances

The administrator facilitates processes and engages in activities insuring that:

A. Knowledge of learning, teaching and student development
   is used to inform management decisions   4 3 2 1 NA
   Formative Indicator   1☐   2☐   3☐   4☐

B. Operational procedures are designed and managed to
   maximize opportunities for successful learning   4 3 2 1 NA
   Formative Indicator   1☐   2☐   3☐   4☐

C. Emerging trends are recognized, studied and applied
   as appropriate   4 3 2 1 NA
   Formative Indicator   1☐   2☐   3☐   4☐

D. Operational plans and procedures to achieve the vision
   and goals of the school are in place   4 3 2 1 NA
   Formative Indicator   1☐   2☐   3☐   4☐

E. Collective bargaining and other contractual agreements
   related to the school are effectively managed   4 3 2 1 NA
   Formative Indicator   1☐   2☐   3☐   4☐

F. The school plant, equipment and support systems operate
   safely, efficiently and effectively   4 3 2 1 NA
   Formative Indicator   1☐   2☐   3☐   4☐

G. Time is managed to maximize attainment of organizational
   goals   4 3 2 1 NA
   Formative Indicator   1☐   2☐   3☐   4☐

H. Potential problems and opportunities are
   Identified   4 3 2 1 NA
   Formative Indicator   1☐   2☐   3☐   4☐

I. Problems are confronted and resolved in a
   timely manner   4 3 2 1 NA
   Formative Indicator   1☐   2☐   3☐   4☐

J. Financial, human and material resources are aligned to the
   goals of schools   4 3 2 1 NA

Formative Indicator   1 ☐   2 ☐   3 ☐   4 ☐

K. The school acts entrepreneurially to support continuous

Improvement   4   3   2   1   NA

Formative Indicator   1 ☐   2 ☐   3 ☐   4 ☐

L. Organizational systems are regularly monitored and

modified as needed   4   3   2   1   NA

Formative Indicator   1 ☐   2 ☐   3 ☐   4 ☐

M. Stakeholders are involved in decisions affecting

schools   4   3   2   1   NA

Formative Indicator   1 ☐   2 ☐   3 ☐   4 ☐

N. Responsibility is shared to maximize ownership and

accountability   4   3   2   1   NA

Formative Indicator   1 ☐   2 ☐   3 ☐   4 ☐

O. Effective problem-framing and problem-solving skills

are used   4   3   2   1   NA

Formative Indicator   1 ☐   2 ☐   3 ☐   4 ☐

P. Effective conflict resolution skills are used   4   3   2   1   NA

Formative Indicator   1 ☐   2 ☐   3 ☐   4 ☐

Q. Effective group-process and consensus building

skills are used   4   3   2   1   NA

Formative Indicator   1 ☐   2 ☐   3 ☐   4 ☐

R. Effective communication skills are used   4   3   2   1   NA

Formative Indicator   1 ☐   2 ☐   3 ☐   4 ☐

S. There is effective use of technology to manage school

operations   4   3   2   1   NA

Formative Indicator   1 ☐   2 ☐   3 ☐   4 ☐

T. Fiscal resources of the school are managed responsibly,

efficiently and effectively   4   3   2   1   NA

Formative Indicator   1 ☐   2 ☐   3 ☐   4 ☐

U. A safe, clean and aesthetically pleasing school environment is created and maintained 4 3 2 1 NA

Formative Indicator 1☐ 2☐ 3☐ 4☐

V. Human resource functions support the attainment of

school goals 4 3 2 1 NA

Formative Indicator 1☐ 2☐ 3☐ 4☐

W. Confidentiality and privacy of school records

are maintained 4 3 2 1 NA

Formative Indicator 1☐ 2☐ 3☐ 4☐

STANDARD THREE COMMENTS

Evaluator Comments   Administrator Comments

_____   _____

_____   _____

_____   _____

STANDARD 4   A school administrator is an educational leader who promotes the success of all students by **collaborating with families and community members, responding to diverse community interests and needs, and mobilizing community resources.**

Evidence that an administrator meets Standard Four is provided by documentation of the following Knowledge, Disposition and Performance criteria. Indicators are listed under each criterion with opportunity for additional evidence to be added. Evidence should be provided in the administrator's portfolio for the evaluator to use in addition to direct observation of educational leadership. The administrator will be evaluated as <u>exceeds, meets, is progressing or falls below</u> performance standards. A mark of one or two will require that a Performance Improvement Plan be completed. (4 = exceeds standards, 3 = meets standards, 2 = progressing to a level of meeting standards consistently, 1 = does not meet standards, and NA = does not apply)

Knowledge

The administrator has knowledge and understanding of:

94

A. Issues and trends that impact the school

community   4 3 2 1 NA

Formative Indicator   1 ☐   2 ☐   3 ☐   4 ☐

B. The conditions and dynamics of the diverse

school community   4 3 2 1 NA

Formative Indicator   1 ☐   2 ☐   3 ☐   4 ☐

C. Community Resources   4 3 2 1 NA

Formative Indicator   1 ☐   2 ☐   3 ☐   4 ☐

D. Community relations, marketing strategies,

and processes   4 3 2 1 NA

Formative Indicator   1 ☐   2 ☐   3 ☐   4 ☐

E. Successful models of school, family, business, community,

government and higher education partnerships   4 3 2 1 NA

Formative Indicator   1 ☐   2 ☐   3 ☐   4 ☐

Dispositions

The administrator believes in, values, and is committed to:

A. Schools operating as an integral part of the larger

community   4 3 2 1 NA

Formative Indicator   1 ☐   2 ☐   3 ☐   4 ☐

B. Collaboration and communication with

families   4 3 2 1 NA

Formative Indicator   1 ☐   2 ☐   3 ☐   4 ☐

C. Involvement of families and other stakeholders in school

decision-making processes   4 3 2 1 NA

Formative Indicator   1 ☐   2 ☐   3 ☐   4 ☐

D. The proposition that diversity enriches the school

         4 3 2 1 NA

Formative Indicator   1 ☐   2 ☐   3 ☐   4 ☐

E. Families as partners in the education of their

children   4 3 2 1 NA

Formative Indicator   1☐ 2☐ 3☐ 4☐

F. Resources of the family and community needing to be
brought to bear on the education of student   4 3 2 1 NA

Formative Indicator   1☐ 2☐ 3☐ 4☐

G. An informed public   4 3 2 1 NA

Formative Indicator   1☐ 2☐ 3☐ 4☐

Performances

The administrator facilitates processes and engages in activities ensuring that:

A. High visibility, active involvement, and communication
with the larger community is a priority   4 3 2 1 NA

Formative Indicator   1☐ 2☐ 3☐ 4☐

B. Relationships with community leaders are identified and
nurtured   4 3 2 1 NA

Formative Indicator   1☐ 2☐ 3☐ 4☐

C. Information about family and community concerns,
expectations, and needs is used regularly   4 3 2 1 NA

Formative Indicator   1☐ 2☐ 3☐ 4☐

D. There is outreach to different business, religious, political,
and service agencies and organizations   4 3 2 1 NA

Formative Indicator   1☐ 2☐ 3☐ 4☐

E. Credence is given to individuals and groups whose values
and opinions may conflict   4 3 2 1 NA

Formative Indicator   1☐ 2☐ 3☐ 4☐

F. The school and community serve one another
as resources   4 3 2 1 NA

Formative Indicator   1☐ 2☐ 3☐ 4☐

G. Partnerships are established with area businesses, institutions
of higher education, and community groups to strengthen
programs and support school goals.   4 3 2 1 NA

Formative Indicator   1☐ 2☐ 3☐ 4☐

96

H. Community youth family services are integrated with
school programs   4 3 2 1 NA
Formative Indicator   1☐   2☐   3☐   4☐

I. Community stakeholders are treated equitably   4 3 2 1 NA
Formative Indicator   1☐   2☐   3☐   4☐

J. Effective media relations are developed and
Maintained   4 3 2 1 NA
Formative Indicator   1☐   2☐   3☐   4☐

K. A comprehensive program of community relations is
established   4 3 2 1 NA
Formative Indicator   1☐   2☐   3☐   4☐

L. Public resources and funds are used
appropriately and wisely   4 3 2 1 NA
Formative Indicator   1☐   2☐   3☐   4☐

M. Community collaboration is modeled for staff   4 3 2 1 NA
Formative Indicator   1☐   2☐   3☐   4☐

N. Opportunities for staff to develop collaborative skills are
provided   4 3 2 1 NA
Formative Indicator   1☐   2☐   3☐   4☐

STANDARD FOUR COMMENTS

Evaluator Comments   Administrator Comments

_____   _____

_____   _____

_____   _____

STANDARD 5   A school administrator is an educational leader who promotes the success of all students by **acting with integrity, fairness, and in an ethical manner.**

Evidence that an administrator meets Standard Five is provided by documentation of the following Knowledge, Disposition and Performance criteria. Indicators are listed under each criterion with opportunity for additional *evidence to be added. Evidence should be provided in the administrator's portfolio for the evaluator to use in addition to direct observation of educational leadership. The administrator will be evaluated as <u>exceeds, meets, is progressing or falls below</u> performance standards. A mark of one or two will require that a Performance Improvement Plan be completed. (4 = exceeds standards, 3 = meets standards, 2 = progressing to a level of meeting standards consistently, 1 = does not meet standards, and NA = does not apply)*

Knowledge

The administrator has knowledge and understanding of:

    A. The purpose of education and the role of leadership in
       modern society   4   3   2   1   NA
       Formative Indicator   1 ☐   2 ☐   3 ☐   4 ☐

    B. Various ethical frameworks and perspectives
       on ethics   4   3   2   1   NA
       Formative Indicator   1 ☐   2 ☐   3 ☐   4 ☐

    C. The values of the diverse school community   4   3   2   1   NA
       Formative Indicator   1 ☐   2 ☐   3 ☐   4 ☐

    D. Professional codes of ethics   4   3   2   1   NA
       Formative Indicator   1 ☐   2 ☐   3 ☐   4 ☐

    E. The philosophy and history of education   4   3   2   1   NA
       Formative Indicator   1 ☐   2 ☐   3 ☐   4 ☐

Dispositions

The administrator believes in, values and is committed to:

    A. The ideal of the common good   4   3   2   1   NA
       Formative Indicator   1 ☐   2 ☐   3 ☐   4 ☐

    B. The principles in the Bill of Rights   4   3   2   1   NA
       Formative Indicator   1 ☐   2 ☐   3 ☐   4 ☐

    C. Bringing ethical principles to the decision-
       making process   4   3   2   1   NA
       Formative Indicator   1 ☐   2 ☐   3 ☐   4 ☐

D. Subordinating one's own interest to the good of the
school community   4 3 2 1 NA

Formative Indicator   1 ☐   2 ☐   3 ☐   4 ☐

E. Accepting the consequences for upholding one's
Principles and action   4 3 2 1 NA

Formative Indicator   1 ☐   2 ☐   3 ☐   4 ☐

F. Using the influence of one's office constructively and
productively in the service of all students and
their families   4 3 2 1 NA

Formative Indicator   1 ☐   2 ☐   3 ☐   4 ☐

G. Development of a caring school community   4 3 2 1 NA

Formative Indicator   1 ☐   2 ☐   3 ☐   4 ☐

Performances

The administrator:

A. Examines personal and professional values   4 3 2 1 NA

Formative Indicator   1 ☐   2 ☐   3 ☐   4 ☐

B. Demonstrates a personal and professional
code of ethics   4 3 2 1 NA

Formative Indicator   1 ☐   2 ☐   3 ☐   4 ☐

C. Demonstrates values, beliefs, and attitudes that inspire
others to higher levels of performance   4 3 2 1 NA

Formative Indicator   1 ☐   2 ☐   3 ☐   4 ☐

D. Serves as a role model   4 3 2 1 NA

Formative Indicator   1 ☐   2 ☐   3 ☐   4 ☐

E. Accepts responsibility for school operations   4 3 2 1 NA

Formative Indicator   1 ☐   2 ☐   3 ☐   4 ☐

F. Considers the impact of one's administrative practices
on others   4 3 2 1 NA

Formative Indicator   1 ☐   2 ☐   3 ☐   4 ☐

G. Uses the influence of the office to enhance the educational program rather than for personal gain   4 3 2 1 NA

Formative Indicator   1☐   2☐   3☐   4☐

H. Treats people fairly, equitably, and with

dignity and respect   4 3 2 1 NA

Formative Indicator   1☐   2☐   3☐   4☐

I. Protects the rights and confidentiality of

students and staff   4 3 2 1 NA

Formative Indicator   1☐   2☐   3☐   4☐

J. Demonstrates appreciation for and sensitivity to the

diversity in the school community   4 3 2 1 NA

Formative Indicator   1☐   2☐   3☐   4☐

K. Opens the school to public scrutiny   4 3 2 1 NA

Formative Indicator   1☐   2☐   3☐   4☐

L. Fulfills legal and contractual obligations   4 3 2 1 NA

Formative Indicator   1☐   2☐   3☐   4☐

STANDARD FIVE COMMENTS

Evaluator Comments   Administrator Comments

_____   _____

_____   _____

_____   _____

STANDARD 6   A school administrator is an educational leader who promotes the success of all students by **understanding, responding to, and influencing the larger political, social, economic, legal, and cultural context.**

Evidence that an administrator meets Standard Six is provided by documentation of the following Knowledge, Disposition and Performance criteria. Indicators are listed under each criterion with opportunity for additional evidence to be added. Evidence should be provided in the administrator's portfolio for the evaluator to use in addition to direct observation of educational leadership. The administrator will be evaluated as exceeds, meets, is progressing or falls below

100

performance standards. A mark of one or two will require that a Performance Improvement Plan be completed. (4 = exceeds standards, 3 = meets standards, 2 = progressing to a level of meeting standards consistently, 1 = does not meet standards, and NA = does not apply)

Knowledge

The administrator has knowledge and understanding of:

    A. Principles of representative governance that under gird

        the system of American schools   4 3 2 1 NA

        Formative Indicator   1 ☐   2 ☐   3 ☐   4 ☐

    B. The role of public education in developing and renewing a

        democratic society and an economically

        productive nation   4 3 2 1 NA

        Formative Indicator   1 ☐   2 ☐   3 ☐   4 ☐

    C. The law as related to education and schooling   4 3 2 1 NA

        Formative Indicator   1 ☐   2 ☐   3 ☐   4 ☐

    D. The political, social, cultural, and economic systems and

        processes that impact schools   4 3 2 1 NA

        Formative Indicator   1 ☐   2 ☐   3 ☐   4 ☐

    E. Models and strategies of change and conflict resolution as

        applied to the larger political, social, cultural and economic

        contexts of schooling   4 3 2 1 NA

        Formative Indicator   1 ☐   2 ☐   3 ☐   4 ☐

    F. Global issues and forces affecting teaching

        and learning   4 3 2 1 NA

        Formative Indicator   1 ☐   2 ☐   3 ☐   4 ☐

    G. The dynamics of policy development and advocacy under

        our democratic political system   4 3 2 1 NA

        Formative Indicator   1 ☐   2 ☐   3 ☐   4 ☐

    H. The importance of diversity and equity in a

        democratic society   4 3 2 1 NA

Formative Indicator   1☐   2☐   3☐   4☐

Dispositions

The administrator believes in, values, and is committed to:

    A. Education as a key to opportunity and

       social mobility   4   3   2   1   NA

       Formative Indicator   1☐   2☐   3☐   4☐

    B. Recognizing a variety of ideas, values,

       and cultures   4   3   2   1   NA

       Formative Indicator   1☐   2☐   3☐   4☐

    C. Importance of a continuing dialogue with other decision

       makers affecting education   4   3   2   1   NA

       Formative Indicator   1☐   2☐   3☐   4☐

    D. Actively participating in the political and policy-making

       context in the service of education   4   3   2   1   NA

       Formative Indicator   1☐   2☐   3☐   4☐

    E. Using legal systems to protect student rights and improve

       student opportunities   4   3   2   1   NA

       Formative Indicator   1☐   2☐   3☐   4☐

Performance

The administrator facilitates processes and engages in activities ensuring that:

    A. The environment in which schools operate is influenced

       on behalf of students and their families   4   3   2   1   NA

       Formative Indicator   1☐   2☐   3☐   4☐

    B. Communication occurs among the school community

       concerning trends, issues, and potential changes in the

       environment in which schools operate   4   3   2   1   NA

       Formative Indicator   1☐   2☐   3☐   4☐

    C. There is ongoing dialogue with representatives of

       diverse community groups   4   3   2   1   NA

       Formative Indicator   1☐   2☐   3☐   4☐

D. The school community works within the framework of
   policies, laws, and regulations enacted by local, state, and
   federal authorities   4 3 2 1 NA
   Formative Indicator   1☐   2☐   3☐   4☐

E. Public policy is shaped to provide quality education
   for students   4 3 2 1 NA
   Formative Indicator   1☐   2☐   3☐   4☐

F. Lines of communication are developed with decision
   makers outside the school community   4 3 2 1 NA
   Formative Indicator   1☐   2☐   3☐   4☐

STANDARD SIX COMMENTS

Evaluator Comments   Administrator Comments

_____   _____

_____   _____

_____   _____

Signatures indicate that the summative evaluation has been reviewed and
discussed. Copies will be provided to the administrator and supervisor.

_____   _____

Evaluator's Signature   Administrator's Signature

_____   _____

Date   Date

PROFESSIONAL REFLECTION SHEET

The Reflection Sheet could be completed by the administrator following formal observations, the completion of the professional development plan, or the completion of the professional improvement plan and taken to the evaluation conference. This form may be used by the administrator and supervisor to discuss and document standards/criteria. It reflects one's own opinion of the professional effort.

Administrator_____Work Site_____

Job Role_____Date_____/_____/_____

1. As I reflect on the formal observation, I have these strengths and concerns:

_____

_____

_____

_____

2. As I reflect on my Professional Development Plan for the year, I have accomplished:_____

_____

_____

_____

3. As I reflect on my Professional Development Plan for the year, I have these concerns:_____

_____

_____

_____

4. As I reflect on my Professional Improvement Plan for the year, I have met my goal by:_____

_____

_____

_____

5. As I reflect on my Professional Improvement Plan for the year, I have
    failed to meet my goal due to:_____

    _____

    _____

    _____

    _____

6. Reflections on my summative evaluation include:_____

    _____

    _____

    _____

    _____

CHAPTER TWO: CERTIFICATED STAFF EVALUATION MODEL

PERFORMANCE-BASED
INSTRUCTIONAL STAFF EVALUATION

PHILOSOPHY

Evaluation is a cooperative and continuous process. It involves professional educators and others, where applicable, for the purpose of improving the quality of instruction and educational activities for the student.

The evaluation process should be implemented in a positive manner; to help the individual being evaluated. Except where required in statute, completed evaluative instruments should be confidential and used by the evaluator and person being evaluated for the purpose of instructional improvement.

PURPOSES

1. To provide assistance to the individual professional in specific tasks for providing better educational opportunities for the student.
2. To help the individual recognize his or her role in the total school program.
3. To identify an individual's strengths and weaknesses.
4. To protect and promote the teaching profession.
5. To provide a record of performance.
6. To assist the process of promotion.
7. To protect the individual from unwarranted criticism.
8. To assist in the process of reassignment.

107

9. To assist in the termination process.

10. To provide material for letters of reference.

PRINCIPLES AND PROCEDURES

Formative Evaluation

The formative evaluation provides opportunity for the evaluator and instructional staff member to discuss the teaching act, student management, classroom climate, differentiation of instruction, and many other topics integral to the execution of quality instruction. The staff member knows exactly what the evaluator is looking for and can execute the rubric established by the district. Formative evaluation also provides time for portfolio sharing and professional development planning.

Summative Evaluation

The summative evaluation is a composite of information including the formative observations as well as other information gathered by the evaluator and provided by the staff member. The summative evaluation should accurately reflect the instruction of the classroom and overall school involvement of the staff member. It may serve as the basis for administrative decision making regarding professional development needs or issuance of contract..

Post Observation Conference

A post observation conference should be conducted within a reasonable period of time following each classroom visitation. This conference should include a discussion of identified strengths and weaknesses.

Performance Improvement Plan

If staff members fall below expectation in any area, Performance Improvement Plans should be developed to allow improvement by the staff member. Teacher performance should be identified; responsibilities of both administrator and teacher for achieving performance improvement should be noted. Feedback should be gathered in accordance with the timeline established in the professional performance improvement plan

Evaluator

The principal of the building is usually the evaluator. However, the use of multiple evaluators may be appropriate and beneficial in certain circumstances.

Appeal Process

Should there be a disagreement concerning the evaluation results, the evaluator may request a conference with the evaluator's immediate supervisor and the evaluator. If the disagreement is not resolved, the policies of the board of education, and grievance procedures for certificated personnel will be followed.

FREQUENCY OF EVALUATION

- A minimum of one summative evaluation per year will be completed for all non-tenured teachers.
- A minimum of one summative evaluation will be completed for all tenured teachers every three years.
- Formative observations used in developing a summative evaluation will occur as frequently as needed.

EVALUATION STANDARDS, CRITERIA AND INDICATORS

INSTRUCTIONAL STAFF

The standards for instructional staff followed by the criteria and indicators of the standard allow the evaluator to follow some specific items that may be considered when completing the evaluation of instructional staff. Additions or deletions should be made to meet the needs of the district.

STANDARD I: INSTRUCTIONAL TECHNIQUES OF THE TEACHER MEET THE NEEDS OF ALL STUDENTS, SUPPORT THE GOALS OF THE DISTRICT, AND REFLECT CURRENT TRENDS.

1.   **Establishing rationale for the lesson and building new concepts and skills upon those the students already have.**

2.   **Refer to the unit objectives and state the specific objectives for the lesson.**

3.   **Provide input opportunities and exhibit proper questioning techniques.**

4. **Model ideal instructional behavior.**

5. **Demonstrates reinforcement of previous learning and checks for comprehension.**

6. **Provide for supervised work and study and the use of technology.**

7. **Summary and assignment.**

STANDARD II: CLASSROOM TECHNIQUES REFLECT QUALITY INSTRUCTIONAL PRACTICES AND PROMOTE THE SUCCESS OF ALL STUDENTS.

1. **Teaching is enthusiastic and businesslike.**

   A. Selects and plans learning experiences on specific objectives.

   B. Maintains effective class control and rapport with the student.

   C. Exhibits positive verbal and nonverbal influences on the student.

   D. Provides an atmosphere in which the student remains at task.

   E. Exhibits fairness and consistency in dealing with behavior problems.

   F. Assumes responsibility for discipline.

   G. Tests are promptly checked and results reported to the student.

2. **Classroom presentation is clear and structured.**

   A. Work is relevant and in sufficient amounts for in-depth learning.

   B. Activities are consistent with lesson objectives.

3. **Learning experiences stimulate student involvement.**

   A. Stimulates and provides opportunities for pupil participation.

   B. Frequently emphasizes success and reinforces positive growth of all learners.

   C. Stimulates interest and develops positive attitudes for learning.

   D. Accepts and utilizes student feedback in instruction.

   E. Provides the student with continuous feedback concerning their performance.

   F. Uses supportive criticism rather than blame, shame, or sarcasm.

110

4. **Learning experiences are applied to everyday living situations**.

   A. Utilizes and builds upon student interest and prior knowledge.

   B. Asks questions which call for more than a recital of facts.

   C. Utilizes community resources in instruction.

   D. Has knowledge of and utilizes community agencies, groups, and individuals to further the educational program.

   E. Assists the student in developing skills for self-evaluation.

   F. Assists the student in gaining knowledge about careers in the curriculum area being taught.

5. **Planning is comprehensive enough to adequately involve each student**.

   A. Provides opportunities for all students to experience success.

   B. Lesson plans are built upon perceivable objectives

   C. Provides the individual student with activities to develop attitudes, appreciations, and values.

   D. Identifies the reasons why the student has or has not met objectives.

   E. Makes clear and reasonable assignments.

6. **Teaching resources conform to the prescribed curriculum**.

   A. Uses adopted textbooks and other resources.

   B. Activities are consistent with lesson objectives.

7. **Teaching resources are related to the student=s interests and abilities**.

   A. Selects instructional materials and provides for learning experiences appropriate to the needs of individuals.

   B. Uses strategies that involve the student in higher levels of thinking.

   C. Uses words and content appropriate to the subject area and the student's abilities.

8. **A variety of teaching resources and methods are used**.

   A. Provides a variety of learning modes.

   B. Plans change in teaching strategies based on the results of assessment.

9. **A variety of techniques to evaluate the student progress are used.**

   A. Provides the student with feedback as they progress toward goals.

   B. Relates test questions and other evaluative procedures to the objectives of the curriculum.

   C. Provides enough valid tests and oral and written exercises to justify marks assigned to pupils.

   D. Phrases questions so that the student may respond with more than a yes or no answer.

   E. Progress reports to parents are effective.

10. **Demonstrates knowledge of subject matter.**

   A. Displays a competent knowledge of curriculum and subject matter.

   B. Selects and presents subject matter that is accurate.

   C. Selects and presents subject matter that is appropriate to the abilities and interests of the student.

STANDARD III: THE CLASSROOM ATMOSPHERE ENCOURAGES THE STUDENTS TO DEVELOP THE KNOWLEDGE, SKILLS AND PROCESSES NEEDED FOR SUCCESS.

1. **Mutual respect between the student and teacher is evident.**

   A. Shows respect for and utilizes pupil opinions and suggestions.

   B. Teacher and students share in the enjoyment of humorous situations.

   C. Interest is shown in all the students.

2. **Self-discipline is stressed in maintaining classroom control.**

   A. Maintains order but allows enough freedom for the student to develop and explore ideas on their own.

   B. Sets example of self-control.

   C. Emphasizes the importance of human rights and responsibilities

   D. Corrects disruptive behavior constructively.

3. **Interference with learning is minimized.**

   A. Displays enthusiasm and vitality in performing the teaching job.

   B. Does not leave class unattended.

   C. Uses class time for worthwhile learning activities.

4. **An attractive learning environment is maintained in the classroom.**

   A. Maintains an attractive classroom setting, utilizing student work, and other displays appropriately.

   B. Gives appropriate attention to keeping litter to a minimum.

   C. Keeps supplies, furnishings, equipment, and interior decorations neatly organized.

5. **Supplies and equipment are utilized with care and responsibility.**

   A. Makes use of bulletin and chalkboards.

   B. Maintains the security of equipment.

   C. Keeps the student abuse of furniture and equipment to a minimum.

STANDARD IV: PROFESSIONALISM IS DEMONSTRATED IN DEALING WITH PEERS, PARENTS, STUDENTS, AND ADMINISTRATORS.

1. **Gives top priority to the welfare of the student.**

   A. Spends adequate time at school for preparation.

   B. Shares responsibilities outside the classroom.

   C. Is available to help the student.

   D. Shows respect for the student.

2. **Shows responsibility to the total school program and community.**

   A. Accepts and reacts to constructive criticism objectively and professionally.

   B. Adheres to official policies and procedures.

   C. Is supportive of school and community activities.

   D. School property is respected as own.

113

3. **Cooperates effectively with colleagues, parents, and community.**

   A. Shows consideration of other teachers in the use of school materials and equipment.

   B. Keeps communication lines open.

   C. Abides by Staff decision.

   D. Responsibly interprets school programs.

4. **Communicates effectively in speaking and writing.**

   A. Seeks to improve own weaknesses.

   B. Formulates clear concise statements

   C. Checks accuracy of evaluations and assignments.

5. **Is ethical in dealing with privileged information.**

   A. Refrains from involving personalities in discussing issues.

   B. Observes the confidentiality of the student and his / her families.

   C. Is concerned with facts vs. hearsay.

6. **Participates in educational activities for self-improvement.**

   A. Participates in and supports professional organizations.

   B. Participates actively in in-service programs

   C. Is a good team worker.

7. **Adequate and accurate records are kept.**

   A. Is aware of student interest, ability, and home background.

   B. Maintains a familiarity with the student=s permanent records.

   C. Maintains written verification of evaluative opinions of the student.

Standard V: **Personal Qualities of the teacher promote the effectiveness of the teacher and the mission and goals of the school/district.**

1. **Is sensitive to human needs.**

   A. Is friendly.

   B. Is willing to listen to and understand other's viewpoints.

C. Maintains congenial and pleasant relationships with fellow workers.

D. Shows tact and courtesy in dealing with others.

E. Does not show prejudice toward others because of race, religion, socio-economic status, ability level, etc.

2. **Exhibits a positive and enthusiastic attitude toward teaching.**

A. Has a sense of humor.

B. Vigorous and original in thought and action.

C. Inspires others to learn.

3. **Proceeds in a rational, self-controlled, mature manner.**

A. Relates well to parents and gains their respect and confidence.

B. Sees whole problems not just parts.

C. Honest, but tactful.

4. **Is punctual in meeting obligations.**

A. Has respect for channels of authority.

B. Maintains good attendance record.

5. **Is neat and well groomed.**

PRE-OBSERVATION

INSTRUCTIONAL STAFF

_____   _____   _____
Teacher   **Date**   **Subject/Grade**

1.   Student homework assignment for the class period:

2.   What are the unit objectives?

What are the specific objectives that will be utilized in the period to be observed?

3.   What teaching materials and methods will be utilized?

4.   Which of the steps of a teaching act will take place?

____   Establishing rationale for the lesson.

____   Refer to the unit objectives and state the specific objectives for the lesson.

____   Provide input opportunities.

____   Model ideal behavior.

____   Reinforcement of previous learning and check for comprehension.

____   Provide for supervised work and study.

116

_____ Summary and assignment.

What other teaching model will be utilized?

5.   What teaching / learning activities will take place?

6.   What particular teaching behaviors do you especially want monitored?

7.   Are there any special circumstances of which the evaluator should be aware?

EVALUATOR'S COMMENTS	TEACHER'S COMMENTS
_____	_____
_____	_____
_____	_____
_____	_____
_____	_____
Evaluator's Signature Date	Teacher's Signature Date

(Signatures simply indicate that this information has been discussed).

Teacher	**Date**	**Subject/Grade**

Time Entered	**Time of Exit**	**Observer**

The principal (supervisor) may use this model for formative evaluation that supports the criteria and indicators of the evaluation model.

1. **Instructional Techniques:**

    _____ Establishing rationale for the lesson building new concepts and skills.

    _____ Refer to the unit objectives and state the specific objectives for the lesson.

    _____ Provide input opportunities and exhibit good questioning techniques.

    _____ Models ideal instructional behavior.

    _____ Demonstrates reinforcement of previous learning and checks for comprehension.

    _____ Provide for supervised work and study and the use of technology.

    _____ Summary and assignment.

2. **Classroom Techniques:**

    _____ Teaching is enthusiastic and businesslike.

    _____ Classroom presentation is clear and structured.

    _____ Learning experiences stimulate the student involvement.

    _____ Learning experiences are applied to every day situations.

    _____ Planning is comprehensive enough to adequately involve each student.

    _____ Teaching resources conform to the prescribed curriculum.

118

_____ Teaching resources are related to the student=s interests and abilities.

_____ A variety of teaching resources and methods are used.

_____ A variety of techniques to evaluate the student progress is used.

_____ Demonstrates a knowledge of subject matter.

3. **Classroom Atmosphere:**

_____ Mutual respect between the student and teacher is evident.

_____ Self-discipline is stressed in maintaining classroom control.

_____ Interference with learning is minimized.

_____ An attractive learning environment is maintained in the classroom.

_____ Supplies and equipment are utilized with care and responsibility.

4. **Professionalism - The Teacher:**

_____ Gives top priority to the welfare of the student.

_____ Shows responsibility to the total school program and community.

_____ Cooperates effectively with colleagues, parents, and community.

_____ Communicates effectively in speaking and writing.

_____ Is ethical in dealing with privileged information.

_____ Participates in educational activities for self-improvement.

_____ Adequate and accurate records are kept.

5. **Personal Qualities - The Teacher:**

_____ Is sensitive to human needs.

_____ Exhibits a positive and enthusiastic attitude toward teaching.

_____ Proceeds in a rationale, self-controlled, mature manner.

_____ Is punctual in meeting obligations.

_____ Is neat and well groomed.

EVALUATOR'S COMMENTS	TEACHER'S COMMENTS
_____	_____
_____	_____
_____	_____
_____	_____

_____ _____
Evaluator's Signature   Date   Instructor's Signature   Date

(Signatures simply indicate that this information has been discussed).

_____   _____
Employee's Name   **Date**

List the objectives for improvement.

What training could you get to help you?

List equipment or materials that would improve your instructional efforts.

List the in-service, training, etc. that you and your supervisor have agreed to in your performance development plan for this school year.

Reflection on the value of the performance development plan.

_____   _____
Supervisor's Signature   Date   Employee's Signature   Date
(Signatures indicate that this information has been discussed.)

PERFORMANCE IMPROVEMENT PLAN

_____   _____
Teacher   **Subject/Grade Level**

_____   _____
Evaluator   **Date**

Place only one improvement criterion per sheet. Use multiple sheets if more than one criterion needs to be improved.

1.   Criterion*:

2.   Improvement Objective(s):

3.   Procedural / Responsibilities for achieving the objective(s):

4.   Completion date for achieving the targeted objective(s):

EVALUATOR COMMENTS

    _____

    _____

    _____

    _____

TEACHER COMMENTS

    _____

    _____

    _____

    _____

_____   _____

Evaluator's Signature   Date   Teacher's Signature   Date

Date Objective Achieved_____Objective not achieved_____

_____   _____

Evaluator's Signature   Date   Teacher's Signature   Date

(Signatures simply indicate that this information has been discussed).

TEACHER NAME   POSITION/GRADE LEVEL

EVALUATOR'S NAME   POSITION   DATE

LEVELS: 4   =   CONSISTENTLY MEETS THE CRITERION

3   =   GENERALLY MEETS THE CRITERION

2   =   SELDOM MEETS THE CRITERION

1   =   DOES NOT MEET THE CRITERION

NA   =   NOT APPLICABLE

MARKS OF 1 OR 2 TRIGGERS THE GENERATION OF AN INSTRUCTIONAL IMPROVEMENT PLAN

STANDARD I: INSTRUCTIONAL TECHNIQUES OF THE TEACHER MEET THE NEEDS OF ALL STUDENTS, SUPPORT THE GOALS OF THE DISTRICT, AND REFLECT CURRENT TRENDS.

CRITERIA   LEVEL

1	Establishes the rationale for the lesson and builds new concepts and skills upon those the students already have	4 3 2 1 NA
2	Refers to the unit objectives and states the specific objectives for the lesson (may provide rubrics)	4 3 2 1 NA
3	Provides input opportunities for students and exhibits proper questioning techniques	4 3 2 1 NA
4	Models ideal instructional behavior	4 3 2 1 NA
5	Demonstrates reinforcement of previous learning and checks for comprehension	4 3 2 1 NA
6	Provides for supervised work and study and facilitates the use of technology	4 3 2 1 NA
7	Summarizes the lesson and clearly makes assignments	4 3 2 1 NA

_____

_____

STANDARD II: **CLASSROOM TECHNIQUES REFLECT QUALITY INSTRUCTIONAL PRACTICES AND PROMOTE THE SUCCESS OF ALL STUDENTS.**

CRITERIA   LEVEL

1	Teaching is enthusiastic and businesslike Formative Indicator A ☐ B ☐ C ☐ D ☐ E ☐ F ☐ G ☐	4 3 2 1 NA
2.	Classroom presentation is clear and structured Formative Indicator A ☐ B ☐	4 3 2 1 NA
3	Learning experiences stimulate student involvement Formative Indicator A ☐ B ☐ C ☐ D ☐ E ☐ F ☐	4 3 2 1 NA
4	Learning experiences are applies to everyday life situations Formative Indicator A ☐ B ☐ C ☐ D ☐ E ☐ F ☐	4 3 2 1 NA
5	Planning is comprehensive enough to adequately involve all students Formative Indicator A ☐ B ☐ C ☐ D ☐ E ☐	4 3 2 1 NA
6	Teaching resources conform to the prescribed curriculum Formative Indicator A ☐ B ☐	4 3 2 1 NA
7	Teaching resources are related to the student's interests and abilities Formative Indicator A ☐ B ☐ C ☐	4 3 2 1 NA
8	A variety of teaching resources and methods are used Formative Indicator A ☐ B ☐	4 3 2 1 NA

9	A variety of techniques to evaluate the student's progress are used Formative Indicator A ☐ B ☐ C ☐ D ☐ E ☐	4 3 2 1 NA
10	Demonstrates a knowledge of subject matter Formative Indicator A ☐ B ☐ C ☐	4 3 2 1 NA

COMMENTS/PORTFOLIO INFORMATION REGARDING STANDARD II:_____

_____

_____

STANDARD III: **THE CLASSROOM ATMOSPHERE ENCOURAGES THE STUDENTS TO DEVELOP THE KNOWLEDGE, SKILLS, AND PROCESSES NEEDED FOR SUCCESS.**

CRITERIA   LEVEL

1	Mutual respect between the student and teacher is evident Formative Indicator A ☐ B ☐ C ☐	4 3 2 1 NA
2.	Self-discipline is stressed in maintaining classroom control. Formative Indicator A ☐ B ☐ C ☐ D ☐	4 3 2 1 NA
3	Interference with learning is minimized Formative Indicator A ☐ B ☐ C ☐	4 3 2 1 NA
4	An attractive learning environment is maintained in the classroom Formative Indicator A ☐ B ☐ C ☐	4 3 2 1 NA
5	Supplies and equipment are utilized with care and responsibility Formative Indicator A ☐ B ☐ C ☐	4 3 2 1 NA

COMMENTS/PORTFOLIO INFORMATION REGARDING STANDARD III:_____

STANDARD IV: PROFESSIONALISM IS DEMONSTRATED IN DEALING WITH PEERS, PARENTS, STUDENTS, AND ADMINISTRTORS.

CRITERIA   LEVEL

1	Gives top priority to the welfare of the student Formative Indicator A☐ B☐ C☐ D☐	4 3 2 1 NA
2.	Shows responsibility to the total school program and community Formative Indicator A☐ B☐ C☐ D☐	4 3 2 1 NA
3	Cooperates effectively with colleagues, parents, and community Formative Indicator A☐ B☐ C☐ D☐	4 3 2 1 NA
4	Communicates effectively in speaking and writing Formative Indicator A☐ B☐ C☐	4 3 2 1 NA
5	Is ethical in dealing with privileged information Formative Indicator A☐ B☐ C☐	4 3 2 1 NA
6	Participates in educational activities for self-improvement Formative Indicator A☐ B☐ C☐	4 3 2 1 NA
7	Adequate and accurate records are kept Formative Indicator A☐ B☐ C☐	4 3 2 1 NA

COMMENTS/PORTFOLIO INFORMATION REGARDING STANDARD IV:_____

STANDARD V: **PERSONAL QUALITIES OF THE TEACHER PROMOTE THE EFFECTIVENESS OF THE TEACHER AND THE MISSION AND GOALS OF THE SCHOOL/DISTRICT.**

CRITERIA   LEVEL

1	Is sensitive to human needs Formative Indicator A ☐ B ☐ C ☐ D ☐ E ☐	4 3 2 1 NA
2.	Exhibits a positive and enthusiastic attitude toward teaching Formative Indicator A ☐ B ☐ C ☐	4 3 2 1 NA
3	Proceeds in a rational, self-controlled, mature manner Formative Indicator A ☐ B ☐ C ☐	4 3 2 1 NA
4	Is punctual in meeting obligations Formative Indicator A ☐ B ☐	4 3 2 1 NA
5	Is neat and well groomed	4 3 2 1 NA

COMMENTS/PORTFOLIO INFORMATION REGARDING STANDARD V:_____

_____

_____

OVERALL COMMENTS

(EVALUATOR)   **(TEACHER)**

_____   _____

_____   _____

_____   _____

_____   _____

_____   _____

EVALUATOR'S SIGNATURE   DATE   **TEACHER'S SIGNATURE   DATE**

(Signatures simply indicate that this information has been discussed)

STANDARD I: MANAGEMENT AND ADMINISTRATION OF THE LIBRARY MEDIA CENTER FOCUSES ON THE BENEFIT OF STUDENTS, ASSISTANCE TO FACULTY, AND OVERALL MISSION AND GOALS OF THE SCHOOL/DISTRICT.

The Librarian:

1. **Recognizes the critical role of information retrieval in the future of education.**

    A. Makes long-range plans which guide the development of the library media center.

    B. Encourages the use of new technologies.

2. **Establishes and maintains an environment in which the student and staff can work at productive levels.**

    A. Develops and implements policies and procedures for the operation of the library media center.

    B. Uses initiative to promote the flexible use of the library media center by individuals, small groups, and large groups for research, browsing, recreational reading, viewing, or listening.

    C. Maintains the library media center in a functional, attractive, and orderly environment conducive to student learning.

    D. Arranges and uses space and facilities in the library media center to support the objectives of the instructional program, providing areas for various types of activities.

    E. Communicates health and safety needs of the library media center to the proper authorities.

    F. Assumes responsibility for proper use and care of library media center facilities, materials, and equipment.

130

3. **Manages student behavior in a constructive manner.**

   A. Promotes appropriate learner behavior.

   B. Encourages student self-direction and responsibility for learning; maintains a productive balance between freedom and control.

   C. Exercises consistency in discipline policies.

   D. Corrects disruptive behavior constructively.

4. **Demonstrates competency in selection, acquisition, circulation, and maintenance of materials and equipment.**

   A. Uses a district-approved selection policy based on state guidelines (e.g., **Learning Resources**, Department of Elementary and Secondary Education, 1975, page 48).

   B. Selects materials and equipment that support the curriculum and promote the schools educational philosophy.

   C. Uses approved business procedures for ordering and receiving materials and equipment.

   D. Classifies, catalogs, processes, and organizes for circulation the educational media and equipment according to professional standards established by AASL, state, and local sources.

   E. Uses clearly stated circulation procedures.

   F. Informs staff and students of new materials and equipment.

   G. Establishes and / or follows procedures for maintenance and repair of media equipment.

   H. Periodically weeds and reevaluates the collection to assure a current, attractive, and well-balanced collection.

   I. Assists in production of materials as feasible.

5. **Prepares statistical records and reports needed to administer the library media center.**

   A. Maintains a current inventory of holdings to assure accurate records.

   B. Prepares and submits to administrators such reports as are needed to promote short- and long-term goals of the library media center.

C. Prepares and submits reports to other officials as requested.

6. **Trains and supervises library media center personnel to perform duties efficiently.**

A. Trains and supervises clerks, aides, student assistants and / or adult volunteers in clerical tasks.

B. Trains and supervises library media center personnel to circulate materials and equipment.

C. Trains and supervises library media center personnel to assist the student and staff in the use of the library media center.

7. **Administers budgets according to needs and objectives of the library media center within administrative guidelines.**

A. Submits budget proposals based on needs and objectives of the library media center.

B. Plans expenditures of allocated funds to meet short- and long-term goals.

C. Keeps accurate records of all disbursements for the library media center.

8. **Evaluates library media center programs, services, facilities, and materials to assure optimum use.**

A. Evaluates programs, services, facilities, and materials informally and formally on a continuous basis, identifying strengths and weaknesses.

B. Provides periodically for evaluation by faculty and students.

C. Develops plans for making changes based on evaluations.

9. **Uses time effectively, efficiently, and professionally.**

A. Prioritizes demands on time to provide maximum support of library media center programs and services.

B. Streamlines or eliminates time-consuming or nonessential routines when possible, without lowering the quality of programs and services.

STANDARD II: THE INSTRUCTIONAL PROCESS OF THE SCHOOL IS SUPPORTED BY THE LIBRARY MEDIA CENTER.

The Librarian:

1. **Exercises leadership and serves as a catalyst in the instructional program.**

    A. Serves as instructional resource consultant and media specialist to teachers and the student.

    B. Uses an appropriate variety of media and teaching techniques in instructional situations.

    C. Provides leadership in using newer technologies for instruction.

    D. Provides in-service training and library media center orientation as needed.

    E. Plans and / or participates in special projects or proposals.

    F. Serves on committees involved with designing learning experiences for the student, curriculum revision, or textbook adoption.

    G. Administers resource sharing, interlibrary loan and / or networking activities.

2. **Plans and implements the library media center program of library media skills.**

    A. Considers long-range objectives when planning instruction appropriate to subject and grade levels.

    B. Develops sequential, short-range objectives that facilitate progress toward defined long-range objectives.

    C. Demonstrates knowledge of the general curriculum and observes recommended steps of teaching when in formal instructional situations.

    D. Plans with teachers to identify and implement the library media center skills curriculum within the classroom curriculum.

    E. Continually instructs students and staff, individually or in groups, in the use of the library media center media and equipment.

F. Encourages independent use of the facility, collection, and equipment by the student and staff.

G. Guides the student and staff in selecting appropriate media from a wide range of learning alternatives.

H. Guides and supervises the student and staff in research activities and in the use of reference materials.

I. Communicates effectively with the student and staff.

3. **Promotes the development of reading skills and reading appreciation.**

A. Conveys enthusiasm for books and reading.

B. Develops activities and / or provides individual guidance to motivate reading.

4. **Supports classroom teachers in their instructional units.**

A. Provides a wide variety of resources and supplementary materials.

B. Assists in choosing and collecting appropriate materials.

C. Cooperatively plans and teaches content appropriate to library media center objectives.

D. Cooperates with teachers in designing and implementing a functional study skills program.

5. **Provides resources for professional growth of faculty and staff.**

A. Identifies and encourages use of materials from the library media center and professional library.

B. Informs staff of new materials, equipment, and research in which they have special interest.

C. Suggests resources outside of the library media center collections.

STANDARD III: * INTERPERSONAL RELATIONSHIPS ARE MAINTAINED IN A WAY THAT ENCOURAGES THE USE OF THE LIBRARY MEDIA CENTER BY STUDENTS AND FACULTY.

The Librarian:

1. **Demonstrates positive interpersonal relations with the student.**

   A. Interacts with the individual student in a mutually respectful and friendly manner.

   B. Strives to be an available personal resource for all the students.

   C. Protects user right to privacy and confidentiality in library media center use.

   D. Demonstrates understanding and acceptance of different views and values.

   E. Gives constructive criticism and praise when appropriate.

2. **Demonstrates positive interpersonal relations with educational staff.**

   A. Initiates interaction with colleagues in planning instructional activities for the student.

   B. Shares ideas and methods with other teachers and staff.

   C. Makes appropriate use of support staff services.

   D. Works cooperatively with the school administration to implement policies and regulations for which the school is responsible.

   E. Informs administrators and / or appropriate personnel of school-related matters.

3. **Demonstrates positive interpersonal relations with parents / patrons.**

   A. Provides a climate that encourages communication between the library media center and parents or patrons.

   B. Cooperates with parents in the best interest of the student.

   C. Supports and participates in parent-teacher activities.

   D. Promotes patron involvement with the library media center.

   E. Handles complaints and / or challenged materials in a firm but friendly

135

manner.

F. Identifies community resource persons who may serve to bring the community into the educational process.

STANDARD IV: PROFESSIONAL RESPONSIBILITIES ARE MAINTAINED IN AN APPROPRIATE AND TIMELY MANNER..

The Librarian:

1. **Participates in professional growth activities.**

   A. Keeps abreast of developments in library science and issues related to teaching.

   B. Demonstrates commitment by participating in professional activities (e.g., professional organizations, coursework, workshops, conferences).

   C. Takes advantage of opportunities to learn from colleagues, students, parents, and the community.

2. **Follows the policies and procedures of the school district.**

   A. Strives to stay informed about policies and regulations applicable to his / her position.

   B. Selects appropriate channels for resolving concerns / problems.

3. **Demonstrates a sense of professional responsibility.**

   A. Completes duties promptly, dependably, and accurately in accordance with established job description.

   B. Demonstrates a responsible attitude for student management throughout the entire building.

PRE-OBSERVATION
SCHOOL LIBRARIAN

The librarian completes this form and discusses content with the evaluator prior to the scheduled observation.

1.   What will be accomplished during this observation time?

2.   Which of the basic goals of the program will be addressed?

3.   What specific activities will take place?

4.   Are there any special circumstances of which the evaluator should be aware?

EVALUATOR'S COMMENTS   LIBRARIAN'S COMMENTS

_____   _____

_____   _____

_____   _____

_____   _____

_____   _____

Evaluator's Signature   Date   Librarian's Signature   Date

(Signatures simply indicate that this information has been discussed)

1. **Management and Administration of the Library Media Center:**

_____ Recognizes the critical role of information retrieval in the future of education.

_____ Establishes and maintains an environment in which the student and staff can work at productive levels.

_____ Manages student behavior in a constructive manner.

_____ Demonstrates competency in selection, acquisition, circulation, and maintenance of materials and equipment.

_____ Prepares statistical records and reports needed to administer the library media center.

_____ Trains and supervises library media center personnel to perform duties efficiently.

_____ Administers budgets according to needs and objectives of the library media center within administrative guidelines.

_____ Evaluates library media center programs, services, facilities, and materials to assure optimum use.

_____ Uses time effectively, efficiently, and professionally.

2. **Instructional Process:**

_____ Exercises leadership and serves as a catalyst in the instructional program.

_____ Plans and implements the library media center program of library media skills.

_____ Promotes the development of reading skills and reading appreciation.

_____ Supports classroom teachers in their instructional units.

_____ Provides resources for professional growth of staff.

3. **Interpersonal Relationships:**

_____ Demonstrates positive interpersonal relations with the student.

_____ Demonstrates positive interpersonal relations with educational staff.

_____ Demonstrates positive interpersonal relations with parents / patrons.

4. **Professional Responsibilities:**

_____ Participates in professional growth activities.

_____ Follows the policies and procedures of the school district.

_____ Demonstrates a sense of professional responsibility.

EVALUATOR'S COMMENTS   **LIBRARIAN'S COMMENTS**

_____   _____

_____   _____

_____   _____

_____   _____

_____   _____

Evaluator's Signature   Date   **Librarian's Signature   Date**

(Signatures simply indicate that this information has been discussed.)

_____ _____

Employee's Name   **Date**

List the objectives for improvement.

What training could you get to help you?

List equipment or materials that would improve your instructional efforts.

List the in-service, training, etc. that you and your supervisor have agreed to in your performance development plan for this school year.

Reflection on the value of the performance development plan.

_____   _____
Supervisor's Signature   Date   Employee's Signature   Date
(Signatures indicate that this information has been discussed.)

PERFORMANCE IMPROVEMENT PLAN
SCHOOL LIBRARIAN

1.   Performance Area:

2.   Criterion*:

3.   Improvement Objective(s):

4.   Procedures for Achieving Objective(s):

5.   Appraisal Method and Target Dates:

143

EVALUATOR'S COMMENTS   **LIBRARIAN'S COMMENTS**

_____   _____
_____   _____
_____   _____
_____   _____

_____   _____
Evaluator's Signature   Date   **Librarian's Signature   Date**

(Signatures simply indicate that this information has been discussed).

LIBRARIAN'S NAME

POSITION/GRADE LEVEL

EVALUATOR'S NAME   POSITION   DATE

LEVELS: 4   =   CONSISTENTLY MEETS THE CRITERION

           3   =   GENERALLY MEETS THE CRITERION

           2   =   SELDOM MEETS THE CRITERION

           1   =   DOES NOT MEET THE CRITERION

         NA   =   NOT APPLICABLE

MARKS OF **1** OR **2** TRIGGERS THE GENERATION OF AN INSTRUCTIONAL IMPROVEMENT PLANS

STANDARD I: THE MANAGEMENT AND ADMINISTRATION OF THE LIBRARY MEDIA CENTER FOCUSES ON THE BENEFIT OF STUDENTS, ASSISTANCE TO FACULTY, AND OVERALL MISSION AND GOALS OF THE SCHOOL/DISTRICT.

CRITERIA   LEVEL

1	Recognizes the critical role of information retrieval in the future of education Indicator A ☐ B ☐	4 3 2 1 NA
2	Establishes and maintains an environment in which the student and staff can work at productive levels Indicator A ☐ B ☐ C ☐ D ☐ E ☐ F ☐	4 3 2 1 NA
3	Manages student behavior in a constructive manner Indicator A ☐ B ☐ C ☐ D ☐	4 3 2 1 NA

4	Demonstrates competency in selection, acquisition, circulation, and maintenance of materials and equipment. Indicator A ☐ B ☐ C ☐ D ☐ E ☐ F ☐ G ☐ H ☐ I ☐	4 3 2 1 NA
5	Prepares statistical records and reports needed to administer the library media center Indicator A ☐ B ☐ C ☐	4 3 2 1 NA
6	Trains and supervises library media center personnel to perform duties efficiently Indicator A ☐ B ☐ C ☐	4 3 2 1 NA
7	Administers budgets according to needs and objectives of the library media center within administrative guidelines Indicator A ☐ B ☐ C ☐	4 3 2 1 NA
8	Evaluates library media center programs, services, facilities, and materials to assure optimum use Indicator A ☐ B ☐ C ☐	4 3 2 1 NA
9	Uses time effectively, efficiently, and professionally Indicator A ☐ B ☐	4 3 2 1 NA

COMMENTS/PORTFOLIO INFORMATION REGARDING STANDARD I:_____

_____

_____

STANDARD II: THE INSTRUCTIONAL PRECESS OF THE SCHOOL IS SUPPORTED BY THE LIBRARY MEDIA CENTER.

CRITERIA   LEVEL

1	Exercises leadership and serves as a catalyst in the instructional program of the school/district Indicator A ☐ B ☐ C ☐ D ☐ E ☐ F ☐ G ☐	4 3 2 1 NA
2.	Plans and implements the library media center program of library media skills Indicator A ☐ B ☐ C ☐ D ☐ E ☐ F ☐ G ☐ H ☐ I ☐	4 3 2 1 NA
3	Promotes the development of reading skills and reading appreciation Indicator A ☐ B ☐	4 3 2 1 NA
4	Supports classroom teachers in their instructional units Indicator A ☐ B ☐ C ☐ D ☐	4 3 2 1 NA
5	Provides resources for professional growth of faculty and staff Indicator A ☐ B ☐ C ☐	4 3 2 1 NA

Comments/Portfolio information regarding standard II:_____

_____

_____

STANDARD III: INTERPERSONAL RELATIONSHIPS ARE MAINTAINED IN WAYS THAT ENCOURAGES THE USE OF THE LIBRARY MEDIA CENTER BY STUDENTS AND FACULTY.

CRITERIA   LEVEL

1	Demonstrates positive interpersonal relationships with the students Indicator A ☐ B ☐ C ☐ D ☐ E ☐	4 3 2 1 NA

147

2.	Demonstrates positive interpersonal relationships with teaching staff and administration Indicator A☐ B☐ C☐ D☐ E☐	4 3 2 1 NA
3	Demonstrates positive interpersonal relationships with parents and district patrons Indicator A☐ B☐ C☐ D☐ E☐ F☐	4 3 2 1 NA

COMMENTS/PORTFOLIO INFORMATION REGARDING STANDARD III:_____

_____

_____

STANDARD IV: PROFESSIONAL RESPONSIBILITIES ARE MAINTAINED IN AN APPROPRIATE AND TIMELY MANNER.

CRITERIA   LEVEL

1	Participates in professional growth activities Indicator A☐ B☐ C☐	4 3 2 1 NA
2.	Follows the policies and procedures of the school/district Indicator A☐ B☐	4 3 2 1 NA
3	Demonstrates a sense of professional responsibility Indicator A☐ B☐	4 3 2 1 NA

COMMENTS/PORTFOLIO INFORMATION REGARDING STANDARD IV:_____

_____

_____

148

OVERALL COMMENTS

(EVALUATOR)   (LIBRARIAN)

_____   _____
_____   _____
_____   _____
_____   _____
_____   _____
_____   _____

_____   _____
EVALUATOR'S SIGNATURE   DATE   LIBRARIAN'S SIGNATURE   DATE

(Signatures simply indicate that this information has been discussed).

STANDARD I: THE SCHOOL COUNSELING PROCESS IS FOCUSED IN WAYS TO PROVIDE BENEFIT TO THE STUDENTS AND STAFF AND PROMOTE THE VISION AND GOALS OF THE SCHOOL/DISTRICT.

The Counselor:

1. **Creates a climate conducive to counseling.**

   A. Displays a nonjudgmental and accepting attitude.

   B. Shows respect for others through active listening.

   C. Maintains the confidentiality of the student interviews.

   D. Provides opportunities for the student to explore problems and weigh alternatives in decision-making.

   E. Encourages the student to set goals and assume responsibility for meeting them.

2. **Employs a variety of effective guidance and counseling procedures.**

   A. Counsels with the student individually.

   B. Counsels with the student in small groups.

   C. Conducts class / large-group sessions on appropriate topics.

   D. Consults with parents and staff.

   E. Provides in-service workshops for interested staff and parents.

3. **Provides for individual differences effectively.**

   A. Responds positively to the student's requests for help.

   B. Provides developmental activities emphasizing positive mental health.

   C. Communicates with the student in a manner appropriate to age and level of understanding.

   D. Uses and interprets cumulative data to assist the student.

   E. Assists in appropriate educational planning and placement with individual students.

   F. Systematically contacts the student who needs assistance.

4. **Displays competent knowledge of guidance and counseling.**

   A. Demonstrates knowledge of child / adolescent growth and development.

   B. Selects and administers appropriate test instruments and uses results appropriately.

   C. Displays knowledge of environmental factors and situations that affect the students behavior and development.

   D. Selects and uses guidance materials appropriate for the abilities and interests of the student.

   E. Communicates knowledge of methods and techniques used to change the student behavior.

5. **Uses guidance and counseling time effectively.**

   A. Allots a realistic amount of time for specified guidance activities.

   B. Is available to the student at appointed times.

   C. Begins activities on time.

   D. Uses time effectively for each designated activity.

6. **Implements guidance programs effectively.**

   A. Implements activities related to career exploration and planning.

   B. Provides activities to assist with educational planning.

   C. Provides opportunities to enhance knowledge of self and others.

   D. Implements additional activities that meet the program objectives.

   E. Provides and implements testing program when appropriate.

7. **Demonstrates the ability to communicate effectively with the student.**

   A. Uses correct oral and written communication.

   B. Uses appropriate vocabulary.

   C. Presents ideas logically.

   D. Gives directions that are clear, concise, and reasonable.

   E. Uses a variety of verbal and nonverbal techniques.

   F. Elicits and responds to questions.

   G. Summarizes effectively.

STANDARD II: THE COUNSELING PROGRAM IS CREATED AND MANAGED TO
PROVIDE STUDENT ASSISTANCE.

The Counselor:

1.   **Organizes a systematic, developmental guidance program.**

   A. Uses formal and informal methods to assess the student needs.

   B. Sets priorities for the guidance and counseling program based on the student needs.

   C. Develops goals and objectives for a comprehensive guidance program.

   D. Determines desired student outcomes based on program goals and objectives.

   E. Develops a sequence of guidance program activities to meet stated goals and objectives.

   F. Communicates information concerning the objectives of the guidance program to the student, staff, and others.

   G. Designs and implements a system for the evaluation of the guidance program.

2.   **Develops a structure for implementing the guidance program.**

   A. Maintains an annual schedule of guidance events as well as a daily activity schedule.

   B. Establishes a referral process for counseling services and disseminates the procedure to staff and the student.

   C. Coordinates and maintains a file of student guidance information including cumulative data, referrals, plans, and goals.

   D. Provides resources and guidance materials to meet program goals.

   E. Keeps an up -to- date listing of referral sources available outside of the school system.

   F. Maintains an attractive and accessible office environment.

   G. Provides informative materials or activities designed to enhance the image of the guidance program.

STANDARD III: INTERPERSONAL RELATIONSHIPS CREATE AN ATMOSPHERE CONDUCIVE TO STUDENT AND STAFF PARTICIPATION.

The Counselor:

1. **Demonstrates positive interpersonal relationship with the student.**

   A. Promotes positive self-image in the student.

   B. Promotes the students' self-control.

   C. Makes an effort to know each student as an individual.

   D. Interacts with the student in a mutually respectful and friendly manner.

   E. Gives constructive criticism and praise when appropriate.

   F. Is reasonably available to all the students.

   G. Acknowledges the rights of others to hold differing views or values.

   H. Demonstrates understanding and acceptance of different racial, ethnic, cultural, and religious groups.

   I. Uses discretion in handling confidential information and difficult situations.

2. **Demonstrates positive interpersonal relationships with teaching staff and administrative staff..**

   A. Works cooperatively with colleagues in planning counseling activities.

   B. Shares ideas, materials, and methods with other staff members.

   C. Makes appropriate use of support staff.

   D. Works cooperatively with the school's administration to implement policies and regulations for which the school is responsible.

   E. Informs administrators and / or appropriate personnel of school-related matters.

3. **Demonstrates positive interpersonal relationship with parents / patrons.**

   A. Cooperates with parents in the best interest of the student.

   B. Provides a climate that opens communication between counselor and parent.

   C. Supports and participates in parent-teacher activities.

D. Promotes patron involvement with school.

E. Initiates communication with parents when appropriate.

STANDARD IV: **PROFESSIONAL RESPONSIBILITIES ARE MAINTAINED TO MEET THE NEEDS OF THE STUDENTS AND PROVIDE A QUALITY COUNSELING PROGRAM.**

The Counselor:

1. **Participates in professional growth activities.**

   A. Demonstrates commitment by participation in professional activities (e.g., professional organizations, course work, workshops, conferences).

   B. Takes advantage of opportunities to learn from colleagues, students, parents, and community.

   C. Keeps abreast of developments in the counseling profession.

2. **Follows the policies and procedures of the school district.**

   A. Strives to stay informed about policies and regulations applicable to his / her position.

   B. Selects appropriate channels for resolving concerns / problems.

   C. Assumes responsibilities outside the counseling center as they relate to the school.

   D. Assumes necessary non-counseling responsibilities.

   E. Exercises responsibility for the student management throughout the entire building.

3. **Demonstrates a sense of professional responsibility.**

   A. Completes duties promptly and accurately.

   B. Is punctual.

   C. Provides accurate data to the school and district as requested for management purposes.

   D. Carries out duties in accordance with established job description.

154

_____   _____

Counselor   **Position**

_____   _____

Evaluator   **Date**

Counselor completes this form and discusses content with administrator prior to scheduled observation.

1.   What will be accomplished during this observation time?

2.   Which of the basic goals of the program will be addressed?

3.   What specific activities will take place?

4.   Are there any special circumstances of which the evaluator should be aware?

EVALUATOR'S COMMENTS

_____
_____
_____
_____

_____
Evaluator's Signature   Date

COUNESLOR'S COMMENTS

_____
_____
_____
_____

_____
Counselor's Signature   Date

(Signatures simply imply that information has been discussed)

FORMATIVE EVALUATION
SCHOOL COUNSELOR

_____	_____	_____
Counselor	**Date**	**Position**

_____	_____	_____
Time Entered	**Exit Time**	**Observer**

The principal (supervisor) may use this model for formative evaluations that support the criteria and indicators of the evaluation model.

1. **The Guidance and Counseling Process:**

   _____ Creates a climate conducive to counseling.

   _____ Employs a variety of effective guidance and counseling procedures.

   _____ Provides for individual differences effectively.

   _____ Displays competent knowledge of guidance and counseling.

   _____ Uses guidance and counseling time effectively.

   _____ Implements guidance programs effectively.

   _____ Demonstrates the ability to communicate effectively with the student.

2. **Guidance Program Management:**

   _____ Organizes a systematic, developmental guidance program.

   _____ Develops a structure for implementing the guidance program.

3. **Interpersonal Relationships:**

   _____ Demonstrates positive interpersonal relations with the student.

   _____ Demonstrates positive interpersonal relations with educational staff.

   _____ Demonstrates positive interpersonal relations with parents / patrons.

4.   **Professional Responsibilities:**

_____   Participates in professional growth activities.

_____   Follows the policies and procedures of the school district.

_____   Assumes responsibilities outside the counseling center as they relate to the school.

_____   Demonstrates a sense of professional responsibility.

EVALUATOR'S COMMENTS   **COUNSELOR'S COMMENTS**

_____   _____

_____   _____

_____   _____

_____   _____

_____   _____

_____   _____

Evaluator's Signature / Date   **Counselor's Signature / Date**

(Signatures simply indicate that this information has been discussed).

PERFORMANCE DEVELOPMENT PLAN

_____   _____

Employee's Name   **Date**

List the objectives for improvement.

What training could you get to help you?

List equipment or materials that would improve your instructional efforts.

List the in-service, training, etc. that you and your supervisor have agreed to in your performance development plan for this school year.

Reflection on the value of the performance development plan.

_____   _____

Supervisor's Signature   Date   Employee's Signature   Date

(Signatures indicate that this information has been discussed.)

PERFORMANCE IMPROVEMENT PLAN
SCHOOL COUNSELOR

_____   _____
Counselor   **Position**

_____   _____
Evaluator   **Date**

1.   Performance Area:

2.   Criterion*:

3.   Improvement Objective(s):

4.   Procedures for Achieving Objective(s):

5.   Appraisal Method and Target Dates:

EVALUATOR'S COMMENTS   **COUNSELOR'S COMMENTS**

_____   _____
_____   _____
_____   _____
_____   _____
_____   _____

Date Objective Achieved_____ **Objective Not Achieved**_____

_____   _____
Evaluator's Signature/Date   **Counselor's Signature/Date**
   (Signatures simply indicate that this information has been discussed.)

COUNSELOR'S NAME	POSITION/GRADE LEVEL

EVALUATOR'S NAME	POSITION	DATE

LEVELS: 4 = CONSISTENTLY MEETS THE CRITERION

3 = GENERALLY MEETS THE CRITERION

2 = SELDOM MEETS THE CRITERION

1 = DOES NOT MEET THE CRITERION

NA = NOT APPLICABLE

MARKS OF 1 OR 2 TRIGGERS THE GENERATION OF AN INSTRUCTIONAL IMPROVEMENT PLANS

STANDARD I: THE SCHOOL COUNSELING PROCESS IS FOCUSED IN WAYS TO PROVIDE BENEFIT TO THE STUDENTS AND STAFF AND PROMOTE THE VISION AND GOALS OF THE SCHOOL/DISTRICT.

CRITERIA   LEVEL

1	Creates a climate conducive to counseling Indicator A☐ B☐ C☐ D☐ E☐	4 3 2 1 NA
2	Employs a variety of effective guidance and counseling procedures Indicator A☐ B☐ C☐ D☐ E☐	4 3 2 1 NA
3	Provides for individual differences effectively Indicator A☐ B☐ C☐ D☐ E☐ F☐	4 3 2 1 NA
4	Displays competent knowledge of guidance and counseling Indicator A☐ B☐ C☐ D☐ E☐	4 3 2 1 NA

5	Uses guidance and counseling time effectively Indicator A ☐ B ☐ C ☐ D ☐	4 3 2 1 NA
6	Trains and supervises library media center personnel to perform duties efficiently Indicator A ☐ B ☐ C ☐ D ☐ E ☐	4 3 2 1 NA
7	Demonstrates the ability to communicate effectively with the student Indicator A ☐ B ☐ C ☐ D ☐ E ☐ F ☐ G ☐	4 3 2 1 NA

COMMENTS/PORTFOLIO INFORMATION REGARDING STANDARD I:_____

STANDARD II: **THE COUNCELING PROGRAM IS CREATED AND MANAGED TO PROVIDE STUDENT ASSISTANCE.**

CRITERIA   LEVEL

1	Organizes a systematic, developmental guidance program Indicator A ☐ B ☐ C ☐ D ☐ E ☐ F ☐ G ☐	4 3 2 1 NA
2.	Develops a structure for implementing the counseling program Indicator A ☐ B ☐ C ☐ D ☐ E ☐ F ☐ G ☐	4 3 2 1 NA

COMMENTS/PORTFOLIO INFORMATION REGARDING STANDARD II:_____

STANDARD III: INTERPERSONAL RELATIONSHIPS ARE MAINTAINED IN WAYS THAT ENCOURAGES THE USE OF THE LIBRARY MEDIA CENTER BY STUDENTS AND FACULTY.

CRITERIA   LEVEL

1	Demonstrates positive interpersonal relationships with the students Indicator A ☐ B ☐ C ☐ D ☐ E ☐ F ☐ G ☐ H ☐ I ☐	4 3 2 1 NA
2.	Demonstrates positive interpersonal relationships with teaching staff and administration Indicator A ☐ B ☐ C ☐ D ☐ E ☐	4 3 2 1 NA
3	Demonstrates positive interpersonal relationships with parents and district patrons Indicator A ☐ B ☐ C ☐ D ☐ E ☐	4 3 2 1 NA

COMMENTS/PORTFOLIO INFORMATION REGARDING STANDARD III:_____

_____

_____

STANDARD IV: PROFESSIONAL RESPONSIBILITIES ARE MAINTAINED TO MEET THE NEEDS OF THE STUDENTS AND PROVIDE A QUALITY COUNSELING PROGRAM.

CRITERIA   LEVEL

1	Participates in professional growth activities Indicator A ☐ B ☐ C ☐	4 3 2 1 NA
2.	Follows the policies and procedures of the school/district Indicator A ☐ B ☐ C ☐ D ☐ E ☐	4 3 2 1 NA
3	Demonstrates a sense of professional responsibility Indicator A ☐ B ☐ C ☐ D ☐	4 3 2 1 NA

COMMENTS/PORTFOLIO INFORMATION REGARDING STANDARD IV:_____

_____

_____

OVERALL COMMENTS

EVALUATOR   **LIBRARIAN**

_____   _____

_____   _____

_____   _____

_____   _____

_____   _____

_____   _____

_____   _____

EVALUATOR'S SIGNATURE   DATE   **LIBRARIAN'S SIGNATURE   DATE**

(Signatures simply indicate that this information has been discussed).

CHAPTER THREE: NON-CERTIFICATED EVALUATION MODEL

PERFORMANCE-BASED
NON-CERTIFICATED STAFF EVALUATION

Effective performance evaluation of non-certificated staff is an essential part of the total instructional program. Food service, custodial/maintenance, bus drivers, school nurses and secretaries are included as non-certificated staff. Performance-based evaluation of non-certificated staff should be a continuous process that relates directly to on-the-job performance. The following performance-based evaluation models were cooperative developed among the board of education, administrators, and non-certificated staff. As other performance-based evaluation models for certificated staff, the evaluative criteria and standards for non-certificated staff must reflect measurable, observable, and definable behavior.

The primary purpose of performance-based non-certificated staff evaluation is to facilitate and improve the learning environment through daily performance. An effective evaluation system should identify non-certificated staffs' strengths and weaknesses and provide direction for maintaining and improving necessary skills through systematic professional development activities.

NON-CERTIFICATED STAFF EVALUATION

PHILOSOPHY

Evaluation is a cooperative and continuous process. It involves: 1) principals as building leaders who realize the importance of non-certificated personnel to the learning climate and activities of the school; 2) usually supervisor of buildings and grounds within the district; and 3) the non-certificated staff member. The purpose of evaluation is to improve the quality of role accomplishment as it relates to the overall benefit of the students and professional staff.

The evaluation process should be implemented in a positive manner to assist the individual being evaluated to improve job performance. The evaluative instruments should be confidential and used by the evaluator and person being evaluated for self-improvement.

PURPOSES

1. To provide assistance to the staff member in specific tasks resulting in an improved learning environment in the school.
2. To assist the individual in recognizing his or her role in the total school program.
3. To identify areas of strength and areas, which need improvement as, they are documented and collaboratively discussed using the evaluation instrument.
4. To assist in the development of a staff development or training program.
5. To promote the value of the job to the building and/or district.
6. To provide a record of performance.
7. To assist the process of promotion and/or merit.
8. To protect the staff member from undocumented or unwarranted criticism.
9. To assist in the process of reassignment and/or the provision of letters of reference.
10. To assist in the termination process.

EVALUATION PROCESS

FREQUENCY

Each non-certificated employee should be evaluated during the first semester of the school year. Following the evaluation, a plan for in-service training should be developed to continue the knowledge development and job skills development of staff. If the evaluation shows any criteria below average, a non-certificated performance improvement plan must be generated for improvement of knowledge and job skills. Any person having a performance improvement plan (PIP) will have a second evaluation before the end of the school year or as needed.

PROCEDURE

Each employee will be provided a copy of the performance report that will serve as a rubric for performance. The frequency of evaluation, the procedure for evaluation, and the philosophy and purposes will be discussed in a professional manner.

It will be explained that the employee has the opportunity to supply the evaluator with information to support his/her accomplishment of each standard, criterion, or indicator. The comments section of the form can be used to document any items the evaluator needs documented or any item the staff member being evaluated would like to document.

The quality of performance will be a mutual decision made following discussion regarding job performance. Should there be a disagreement, the evaluator will mark the performance report and employee comments can be written at the end of the report. Continued failure of the employee to remove below average performance may result in termination of employment.

The supervisor and the employee should sign the report following the conference where information is shared between the evaluator and the employee. Signatures do not indicate agreement. They simply indicate that the performance report has been discussed.

The principal should forward a copy of the performance report to district level supervisors if they exist within the district administration.

169

Standard One: **The employee demonstrates quality work in a timely and safe manner.**

1. The employee is accurate and thorough when accomplishing daily job duties.

2. The employee uses time well, is punctual and is able to accomplish daily tasks as well as other jobs that need to be done.

3. Careful attention is given to safety procedures to ensure the safety of the employee, the safety of students, and the safety of the staff in the building.

Standard Two: **The employee demonstrates interest in accomplishing the job in an exemplary manner and shows an eagerness to learn new ideas and techniques regarding the job.**

1. The employee is interested in the job and shows desire to achieve a quality school environment.

2. The employee demonstrates a willingness to change techniques and routines as needed to do the best job possible.

3. Attention is given to keeping the school and work areas neat and free of unnecessary materials.

Standard Three: **The employee demonstrates a proper personal appearance.**

1. Careful attention is given to being neat and clean on the job.

2. The employee exhibits a well-groomed appearance on the job.

170

Standard Four: **The employee demonstrates good interpersonal skills.**

1. The employee demonstrates a "team player" attitude at the school by showing a willingness to assist others and to ability to get along with other workers.

2. Good public relations skills are exhibited with teachers, students, and parents at the school.

3. Cooperation with the supervisor is exhibited in all situations.

Standard Five: **The employee demonstrates leadership among peers and in taking on responsibility of the job.**

1. Leadership is positive and productive and upholds policies.

2. The employee takes responsibility for the job and well-being of the school and students.

Employee's Name   **Date**

List the jobs you would like to be able to improve.

What training could you get to help you?

List equipment or materials that would improve your job efforts.

List the in-service, training, etc. that you and your supervisor have agreed to in your performance development plan for this school year.

172

Reflection on the value of the performance development plan.

_____   _____
Supervisor's Signature   Date   Employee's Signature   Date

(Signatures simply indicate that this information has been discussed.)

_____   _____

Employee's Name   **Date**

Standard/Criterion identified as below average

Action steps to be taken to produce improved performance

Evidence of improved job performance related to the below average
standard/criterion

Plans regarding the ability to maintain improved performance along with other job duties.

_____   _____
Supervisor's Signature   Date   Employee's Signature   Date
(Signatures simply indicate that this information has been discussed)

EMPLOYEE PERFORMANCE REPORT

SCHOOL NURSES

| Nurse's Name | Date |

| Evaluator's Name | Position / School |

Evaluation Procedure

1. The supervisor will rate the employee on each item with a check mark by the appropriate descriptor for each desired quality.
2. The report will be discussed with the employee and signatures of both the employee and the supervisor indicate only that the report was discussed.
3. A copy of the report should be sent to central office to be placed in the employee's file.

Desired Qualities

1. Quality of Work   _____   Accurate and thorough

    _____   Average

    _____   Needs improvement

Comments:

_____

_____

_____

2. Actual Work / Time Utilization   _____   Uses time wisely, remains on task, is punctual

    _____   Average

    _____   Needs improvement

Comments:

_____

_____

_____

3. Work Habits / Safety _____ Resourceful & consistently promotes safety

_____ Average

_____ Needs improvement

Comments:

_____

_____

_____

4. Interest / Achievement_____ Looks for work

_____ Average

_____ Needs improvement

Comments:

_____

_____

_____

5. Adaptability _____ Learns new job demands

_____ Average

_____ Needs improvement

Comments:

_____

_____

_____

6. Neatness _____ Work area/paperwork neat

_____ Average

_____ Needs improvement

Comments:

_____

_____

_____

7.   Personal Appearance _____   Well-groomed/professional

                        _____   Average

                        _____   Needs improvement

     Comments:

     _____

     _____

     _____

8.   Working with Others _____   Works well with others/team

                        _____   Average

                        _____   Needs improvement

     Comments:

     _____

     _____

     _____

9.   Public Relations   _____   Good/courteous/helpful

                        _____   Average

                        _____   Needs improvement

     Comments:

     _____

     _____

     _____

10. Cooperation with Supervisor _____   Always good

                        _____   Average

                        _____   Needs improvement

     Comments:

     _____

     _____

     _____

11. Monitors records and _____   Upholds policies / makes
     students' health   referrals when needed

                         _____   Average

                         _____   Needs improvement

     Comments:

     _____

     _____

     _____

EVALUATOR'S COMMENTS   **NURSE'S COMMENTS**

_____   _____

_____   _____

_____   _____

_____   _____

_____   _____

_____   _____

_____   _____

_____   _____

Evaluator's Signature   Date   Nurse's Signature   Date
(Signatures simply imply that information has been discussed.)

PERFORMANCE STANDARDS AND CRITERIA
CUSTODIAL/MAINTENANCE EMPLOYEES

Standard One: **The employee demonstrates quality work in a timely and safe manner.**

1. The employee is accurate and thorough when accomplishing daily job duties.
2. The employee uses time well and is able to accomplish daily tasks as well as other jobs that need to be done.
3. Careful attention is given to safety procedures to ensure the safety of the employee, the safety of students, and the safety of the staff in the building.

Standard Two: **The employee demonstrates interest in accomplishing the job in an exemplary manner and shows an eagerness to learn new ideas and techniques regarding the job.**

1. The employee is interested in the job and shows desire to achieve a quality school environment.
2. The employee demonstrates a willingness to change techniques and routines as needed to do the best job possible.
3. Attention is given to keeping the school and work areas neat and free of unnecessary materials.

Standard Three: **The employee demonstrates a proper personal appearance.**

1. Careful attention is given to being neat and clean on the job.
2. The employee exhibits a well-groomed appearance on the job.

180

Standard Four: **The employee demonstrates good interpersonal skills.**

1. The employee demonstrates a "team player" attitude at the school by showing a willingness to assist others and to ability to get along with other workers.

2. Good public relations skills are exhibited with teachers, students, and parents at the school.

3. Cooperation with the supervisor is exhibited in all situations.

Standard Five: **The employee demonstrates leadership among peers and in taking on responsibility.**

1. When working in crews or with peers, leadership is positive and productive.

2. The employee takes responsibility for the job and well-being of the school.

_____   _____

Employee's Name   **Date**

List the jobs you would like to be able to improve.

What training could you get to help you?

List equipment or materials that would improve your job efforts.

List the in-service, training, etc. that you and your supervisor have agreed to in your performance development plan for this school year.

Reflection on the value of the performance development plan.

_____   _____

Supervisor's Signature   Date   Employee's Signature   Date

(Signatures simply indicate that this information has been discussed.)

Employee's Name   **Date**

Standard/Criterion identified as below average

Action steps to be taken to produce improved performance

Evidence of improved job performance related to the below average standard/criterion

Plans regarding the ability to maintain improved performance along with other job duties.

_____   _____

Supervisor's Signature   Date   Employee's Signature   Date
(Signatures simply indicate that this information has been discussed)

PERFORMANCE EVALUATION
CUSTODIAL/MAINTENANCE

Employee's Name	**Building**	**Date**

Evaluator's Name	**Evaluator's Title**

Evaluation Procedure

1. The supervisor will rate the employee on each item with a circle and share the rating with the employee at the evaluation conference.

2. Both the employee and the supervisor should sign the report.

3. A copy of the report should be sent to the Supervisor of Buildings and Grounds.

Desired Qualities

1. **Quality of Work:** _____ Accurate and thorough

    _____ Average

    _____ Needs Improvement

    COMMENTS:

    _____

    _____

    _____

2. **Actual Work, Time Utilization**_____ Unusual production

    _____ Average

    _____ Low production

    COMMENTS:

    _____

    _____

    _____

3. **Work Habits / Safety**   _____   Resourceful

                                    _____   Average

                                    _____   Inconsistent

    COMMENTS:

    _____

    _____

4. **Interest / Achievement**   _____   Looks for work

                                    _____   Average

                                    _____   Avoids extra work

    COMMENTS:

    _____

    _____

5. **Adaptability**   _____   Learns new routines

                                    _____   Average

                                    _____   Finds change hard

    COMMENTS:

    _____

    _____

6. **Neatness**   _____   Very neat

                                    _____   Average

                                    _____   Somewhat lacking

    COMMENTS:

    _____

    _____

7. **Personal Appearance** _____ Well-groomed

_____ Average

_____ Careless grooming

COMMENTS:

_____

_____

_____

8. **Working with Others** _____ Good Team Player

_____ Average

_____ Works Best Alone

COMMENTS:

_____

_____

_____

9. **Public Relations -** _____ Always good

Teacher / Pupils _____ Average

_____ Occasional problems

COMMENTS:

_____

_____

_____

10. **Cooperation with Superior** _____ Always good

_____ Average

_____ Lacking

COMMENTS:

_____

_____

_____

11. **Leadership** _____ Strong

_____ Average

_____ Lacking

COMMENTS:

_____

_____

_____

EVALUATOR'S COMMENTS   **CUSTODIAN COMMENTS**

_____   _____

_____   _____

_____   _____

_____   _____

_____   _____

_____   _____

_____   _____

_____   _____

Evaluator's Signature   Date   **Employee's Signature   Date**

(Signatures simply indicate that this information has been discussed.)

Standard One: **The employee demonstrates quality work in a timely and accurate manner.**

1. The employee is accurate and thorough when accomplishing daily job duties.

2. The employee uses time well and is able to accomplish daily tasks as well as meet deadlines under pressure.

3. Careful attention is given to communication procedures to ensure the safety of the school and a pleasant and efficient atmosphere.

Standard Two: **The employee demonstrates interest in accomplishing the job in an exemplary manner and shows an eagerness to learn new ideas and techniques regarding the job.**

1. The employee is interested in the job and shows desire to achieve a quality school environment.

2. The employee demonstrates a willingness to change techniques and routines as needed to do the best job possible.

3. Attention is given to keeping the school and work areas neat and free of unnecessary materials.

Standard Three: **The employee demonstrates a proper personal appearance.**

1. Careful attention is given to being neat and clean on the job.

2. The employee exhibits a well-groomed appearance on the job.

<u>Standard Four</u>:	**The employee demonstrates good interpersonal skills.**

1. The employee demonstrates a "team player" attitude at the school by showing a willingness to assist others and the ability to get along with other workers.
2. Good public relations skills are exhibited with teachers, students, and parents at the school.
3. Cooperation with the supervisor is exhibited in all situations.

<u>Standard Five</u>:	**The employee demonstrates leadership among peers and in taking on responsibility.**

1. When working in teams or with peers, leadership is positive and productive and the employee knows when to take charge.
2. The employee takes responsibility for the job and well-being of the school and maintains confidentiality steadfastly.

---------------------------------   ---------------------------------

Employee's Name   **Date**

List the jobs you would like to be able to improve.

What training could you get to help you?

List equipment or materials that would improve your job efforts.

List the in-service, training, etc. that you and your supervisor have agreed to in your performance development plan for this school year.

Reflection on the value of the performance development plan.

_____   _____

Supervisor's Signature   Date   Employee's Signature   Date

(Signatures simply indicate that this information has been discussed.)

_____   _____

Employee's Name   **Date**

Standard/Criterion identified as below average

Action steps to be taken to produce improved performance

Evidence of improved job performance related to the below average standard/criterion

Plans regarding the ability to maintain improved performance along with other job duties.

_____   _____

Supervisor's Signature   Date   Employee's Signature   Date

(Signatures simply indicate that this information has been discussed)

PERFORMANCE REPORT
CLERICAL/AIDES

Name of Employee   **Building**

Evaluation Procedure

1. The supervisor will rate the employee on each item with a circle and share the rating with the employee at the evaluation conference.
2. Both the employee and the supervisor should sign the report.
3. A copy of the report should be sent to the employee's supervisor to be placed in the employee's file.

Desired Qualities

1. **Quality of Work:**   _____   Accurate and thorough

                               _____   Average

                               _____   Needs Improvement

    COMMENTS:

    _____

    _____

2. **Responsible,**   _____   Works well under pressure

    meets deadlines

                               _____   Average

                               _____   Deadlines aren't met

    COMMENTS:

    _____

    _____

3. **Phone and personal contacts** _____   Consistently quality

    are handled pleasantly and _____   Average

    effectively   _____   Inconsistent

COMMENTS:

_____

_____

_____

4. **Interest / Achievement**   _____   Looks for work

    _____   Average

    _____   Avoids extra work

    COMMENTS:

    _____

    _____

    _____

5. **Knowledge of the**   _____   Learns new routines

    job duties and adaptability   _____   Average

    _____   Finds change hard

    COMMENTS:

    _____

    _____

    _____

6. **Neatness is displayed**   _____   Very neat

    in the work area and   _____   Average

    records kept   _____   Somewhat lacking

    COMMENTS:

    _____

    _____

    _____

7. **Personal Appearance**   _____   Well-groomed

    _____   Average

    _____   Careless grooming

COMMENTS:

_____

_____

_____

8.   **Working with Others**   _____   Good Team Player

                                                              _____   Average

                                                              _____   Works Best Alone

    COMMENTS:

_____

_____

_____

9.   **Public Relations:**   _____   Always good, positive

    Teachers / Pupils / Parents _____   Average

                                                              _____   Occasional problems

    COMMENTS:

_____

_____

_____

10.   **Cooperation with Supervisor**   _____   Always good

                                                              _____   Average

                                                              _____   Lacking

    COMMENTS:

_____

_____

_____

11.   **Leadership and confidentiality**   _____   Strong

    (knows when to take charge and   _____   Average

    avoids gossip)   _____   Lacking

COMMENTS:

_____

_____

_____

EVALUATOR'S COMMENTS   **EMPLOYEE'S COMMENTS**

_____   _____

_____   _____

_____   _____

_____   _____

_____   _____

_____   _____

_____   _____

_____   _____
Evaluator's Signature   Date   Employee's Signature   Date

(Signatures simply indicate that this information has been discussed.)

Standard One: **The employee demonstrates quality work in a timely and safe manner.**

1. The employee is accurate and thorough when accomplishing pre-trip inspections of the bus..

2. The employee uses the seat belt appropriately to ensure safety.

3. Careful attention is given to the cleanliness and condition of the interior of the bus.

Standard Two: **The employee demonstrates interest in accomplishing the job in an exemplary manner and shows an eagerness to maintain safety at all times.**

1. The employee is interested in maintaining the bus in top condition and keeps mileage records accurately.

2. The employee keeps accurate records of time spent driving and on trips.

3. Attention is given to keeping the bus under control at safe and appropriate speeds at all times.

Standard Three: **The employee demonstrates proper bus stop technique for student loading and unloading..**

1. Careful attention is given to the proper use of warning lights.

2. The employee demonstrates proper stopping and starting procedures to allow students to load and/or unload

3. The driver maintains eye contact with students as they enter and exit the bus.

4. Student departure is monitored by the driver and bus start-up only occurs after students are clear of the street.

200

Standard Four: **The employee demonstrates good interpersonal skills with the students as student safety is maintained.**

1. The employee ensures that students are seated while the bus is in motion.

2. Mirrors and cameras are used to ensure student and travel safety..

3. Student control is enhanced by using a seating chart, keeping feet out of the isle, having students face the front, and keeping noise to a minimum.

Standard Five: **The employee demonstrates a good attitude as a part of the school team.**

1. A positive, professional attitude is maintained by the driver.

PERFORMANCE DEVELOPMENT PLAN
BUS DRIVERS

_____   _____

Employee's Name   **Date**

List the jobs you would like to be able to improve.

What training could you get to help you?

List equipment or materials that would improve your job efforts.

List the in-service, training, etc. that you and your supervisor have agreed to in your performance development plan for this school year.

Reflection on the value of the performance development plan.

_____   _____

Supervisor's Signature   Date   Employee's Signature   Date

(Signatures simply indicate that this information has been discussed.)

Employee's Name   **Date**

Standard/Criterion identified as below average

Action steps to be taken to produce improved performance

Evidence of improved job performance related to the below average standard/criterion

Plans regarding the ability to maintain improved performance along with other job duties.

_____   _____
Supervisor's Signature   Date   Employee's Signature   Date
(Signatures simply indicate that this information has been discussed)

Name of Driver   **Bus #**   **Route #**

Evaluation Procedure

1. The supervisor will rate the driver on each item that is checked and share the rating with the driver at the evaluation conference.

2. Both the driver and the supervisor should sign the report.

3. A copy of the report should be sent to the employee's personnel file.

Desired Qualities

1. **Pre-trip inspection** _____ Accurate and thorough

    _____ Average

    _____ Needs Improvement

    COMMENTS:

    _____

    _____

2. **Driver's Seat Belt** _____ Exemplary Use

    _____ Average

    _____ Needs Improvement

    COMMENTS:

    _____

    _____

3. **Interior of Bus** _____ Clean, well kept

    _____ Average

    _____ Needs Improvement

COMMENTS:

_____

_____

4. **Mileage**   _____   Keeps Excellent Record

                           _____   Average

                           _____   Needs Improvement

    COMMENTS:

_____

_____

5. **Time**   _____   Keeps Accurate Record

                           _____   Average

                           _____   Needs Improvement

    COMMENTS:

_____

_____

6. **Speed**   _____   Observes Limits/Safe

                           _____   Average

                           _____   Needs Improvement

    COMMENTS:

_____

_____

7. **Use of warning lights**   _____   Appropriate/Excellent

                           _____   Average

                           _____   Needs Improvement

COMMENTS:

_____

_____

_____

8. **Makes proper stops**   _____   Excellent/Safe

                                  _____   Average

                                  _____   Needs Improvement

    COMMENTS:

    _____

    _____

    _____

9. **Eye contact with students**_____   Always Maintains/Safe

                                  _____   Average

                                  _____   Needs Improvement

    COMMENTS:

    _____

    _____

    _____

10. **Student Departure**   _____   Requires proper exit

                                  _____   Average

                                  _____   Needs Improvement

    COMMENTS:

    _____

    _____

    _____

11. **Bus start-up after stop**   _____   Students Clear Street

                                  _____   Average

                                  _____   Needs Improvement

COMMENTS:

_____

_____

_____

12. **Students are seeated**   _____   Always while in motion

                              _____   Average

                              _____   Needs Improvement

COMMENTS:

_____

_____

13. **Use of mirrors**   _____   Always appropriate

                              _____   Average

                              _____   Needs Improvement

COMMENTS:

_____

_____

14. **Student control: seating chart**_____   Uses appropriately

                              _____   Average

                              _____   Needs Improvement

Student control: feet out of isle_____   Enforces bus Rules

                              _____   Average

                              _____   Needs Improvement

Student control: facing front_____   Enforces bus Rules

                              _____   Average

                              _____   Needs Improvement

Student control: Noise _____ Maintains low Noise

_____ Average

_____ Needs Improvement

COMMENTS:

_____

_____

_____

15. **Driver attitude** _____ Positive/Professional

_____ Average

_____ Needs Improvement

COMMENTS:

_____

_____

_____

EVALUATOR'S COMMENTS   **BUS DRIVER'S COMMENTS**

_____   _____

_____   _____

_____   _____

_____   _____

_____   _____

_____   _____

_____   _____

_____   _____

Evaluator's Signature   Date   **Driver's Signature   Date**

(Signatures simply indicate that this information has been discussed.)

210

Standard One: **The employee demonstrates quality work in a timely and safe manner.**

1. The employee is accurate and thorough when accomplishing daily job duties.

2. The employee uses time well and is able to accomplish daily tasks as well as other jobs that need to be done.

3. Careful attention is given to safety procedures to ensure the safety of the employee, the safety of students, and the safety of the staff in the building.

Standard Two: **The employee demonstrates interest in accomplishing the job in an exemplary manner and shows an eagerness to learn new ideas and techniques regarding the job.**

1. The employee is interested in the job and shows desire to achieve a quality school environment.

2. The employee demonstrates a willingness to change techniques and routines as needed to do the best job possible.

3. Attention is given to keeping the school and work areas neat and free of unnecessary materials.

Standard Three: **The employee demonstrates a proper personal appearance.**

1. Careful attention is given to being neat and clean on the job.

2. The employee exhibits a well-groomed appearance on the job.

Standard Four: **The employee demonstrates good interpersonal skills.**

1. The employee demonstrates a "team player" attitude at the school by showing a willingness to assist others and to ability to get along with other workers.

2. Good public relations skills are exhibited with teachers, students, and parents at the school.

3. Cooperation with the supervisor is exhibited in all situations.

Standard Five: **The employee demonstrates leadership among peers and in taking on responsibility.**

1. When working in crews or with peers, leadership is positive and productive.

2. The employee takes responsibility for the job and well-being of the school.

PERFORMANCE DEVELOPMENT PLAN
FOOD SERVICE

_____   _____
Employee's Name   **Date**

List the jobs you would like to be able to improve.

What training could you get to help you?

List equipment or materials that would improve your job efforts.

List the in-service, training, etc. that you and your supervisor have agreed to in your performance development plan for this school year.

Reflection on the value of the performance development plan.

_____   _____
Supervisor's Signature   Date   Employee's Signature   Date

(Signatures simply indicate that this information has been discussed.)

_____   _____

Employee's Name   **Date**

Standard/Criterion identified as below average

Action steps to be taken to produce improved performance

Evidence of improved job performance related to the below average standard/criterion

<u>Plans regarding the ability to maintain improved performance along with other job duties.</u>

_____   _____
Supervisor's Signature   Date   Employee's Signature   Date
(Signatures simply indicate that this information has been discussed)

PERFORMANCE REPORT
FOOD SERVICE

Name of Employee   **Building**

luation Procedure:

    The Food Service Director and/or the Kitchen Manager will rate the employee on
each item with a check and share the rating with the employee at the evaluation
conference.
Both the employee and the Manager should sign the report.
The report will be filed in the office of the Food Service Director.

red Qualities

Quality of Work: _____   Accurate and thorough
                                       _____   Average
                                       _____   Needs improvement

COMMENTS:

_____
_____
_____

Actual Work, Time Utilization   _____   Unusual production
                                         _____   Average
                                         _____   Needs improvement

COMMENTS:

_____
_____
_____

Work Habits / Safety   _____   Resourceful
                                         _____   Average
                                         _____   Needs improvement
COMMENTS:

_____
_____
_____

Interest / Achievement   _____   Looks for work

_____   Average

_____   Needs improvement

COMMENTS:

_____

_____

_____

Adaptability   _____   Learns new routines

_____   Average

_____   Needs improvement

COMMENTS:

_____

_____

_____

Neatness   _____   Very neat

_____   Average

_____   Needs improvement

COMMENTS:

_____

_____

_____

Personal Appearance   _____   Well-groomed

_____   Average

_____   Needs improvement

COMMENTS:

_____

_____

_____

Working with others   _____   Good team player

_____   Average

_____   Needs improvement

COMMENTS:

_____

_____

_____

Public Relations: Teacher/Pupil   _____   Always good

_____   Average

_____   Needs improvement

COMMENTS:

_____
_____
_____

10. **Cooperation with Supervisor**   _____   Always good
                                        _____   Average
                                        _____   Needs improvement
    COMMENTS:

_____
_____
_____

11. **Leadership**   _____   Positive and strong
                                        _____   Average
                                        _____   Needs improvement
    COMMENTS:

_____
_____
_____

EVALUATOR'S COMMENTS   **EMPLOYEE'S COMMENTS**

_____   _____
_____   _____
_____   _____
_____   _____
_____   _____

_____   _____
Evaluator's Signature   Date   Employee's Signature   Date

(Signatures simply indicate that this information has been discussed.)

APPENDIX A

PORTFOLIO POLICIES AND PROCEDURES
FOR
PERFORMANCE-BASED ADMINISTRATOR EVALUATION

In partial fulfillment of the Performance-Based Administrator Evaluation, the administrator must complete a portfolio reflecting the proposed activities found in sections 3, 4, and 5. The Performance-Based Administrator Evaluation is also based on the possession of knowledge and/or competency in several areas. The administrator should work closely with his/her supervisor(s) to determine the experiences, which will be most beneficial for the administrator. Also the selection of appropriate electives, where possible, can aid this process significantly.

The intent of the portfolio is to provide the administrator the opportunity to document experiences centering on the daily administration and supervisory duties of the administrator/director. The administrator will be expected to complete all projects in section 4.0, (page 4) and ten (10) projects selected from section 5.0 Skill Building Projects, page 6 (all projects identified with an (*) will be required).

1. Introduction: A successful Performance-Based Administrator Evaluation requires the professional commitment of two parties: the administrator that will be evaluated, and the supervisor that will be doing the evaluation.

2.   Purposes: The ultimate goal of the Performance-Based Administrator Evaluation is to enable the evaluator to evaluate the administrator's performance with a high degree of knowledge and confidence, and to assist the administrator in developing his/her professional development plan.

2.1   The breadth of the administrator's portfolio will give the evaluator an understanding of the key aspects of the school administrator's yearly performance.

2.2   The hands-on learning experiences will promote skill building in carrying out key functions performed as an administrator.

221

2.3 The reflective thought component of the portfolio experience will bring insight into purposes, practices, politics and power as played out in school administration.

3.0 **General Expectations and Portfolio Process:** Three components are present in a successful evaluation: observation, communication, and guided reflection.

3.1 The evaluator should be afforded an opportunity by the administrator to shadow him/her while he/she carries out position responsibilities.

3.2 Regular opportunities should be afforded the administrator to interact with teachers, students, parents, and state department of education. division of family services, juvenile officer, police, county court, city and/or county government, and district level personnel including the superintendent as well as maintenance, human resources, support services, and community education services staff. The administrator should participate, as appropriate, in administrative team meetings at the district and building levels as well as meetings of the faculty, parent advisory group, student council and other public forums which will provide a realistic and candid view of the administrator.

3.3 The administrator should be exposed to---and become involved in- --both the routine functions of the office of principal/director/superintendent and specific responsibilities in the areas of communications, business operations, employee relations, public relations, curriculum, facilities management, transportation, food service, and human resources management.

3.4 Begin the Performance-Based Administrator Evaluation and portfolio by the 1st of August or earlier. The evaluator should shadow the administrator prior to the beginning of the school year to gain a perspective of the projects, which need to be done. The bulk of the portfolio and evaluation activities will be during the school year.

3.5 The **portfolio** consists of projects that are designed to enable the administrator to focus on specific areas of school leadership. Over the duration of the **portfolio** development, the administrator will collect a variety of written artifacts (e.g., memos, letters, manuals, data sheets, etc.) that provide evidence of important aspects of school leadership. Then the administrator will **select** from this collection a limited number of artifacts that provide the richest evidence of the work described in that project. The administrator will use these artifacts to support the projects completed during the portfolio portion of the Performance-Based Administrator Evaluation. Later the administrator will **reflect** on the ways in which the responses to the projects and artifacts, taken together, help to document and further define the administrator's professional responsibilities.

3.6 All of the instructions that you will need to complete the portfolio will be found in the **Portfolio Policies and Procedures** materials and in the projects themselves. It is extremely important that the administrator read **ALL** the materials presented in this package before he/she begin the task of collecting documents and assembling the portfolio. The administrator will find the **following** steps are critical for the successful completion of the portfolio. Remember the projects in section 4.1-4.4 and those projects identified with (*) in section 5 are required. Except for those that are required, the administrator may change his/her selection during the process. Read over all directions before beginning and clarify any questions or concerns you may have. Develop a time-line and calendar to ensure that all projects are fully completed within the allotted time period. Develop a plan to collect, file, organize, and label all potential *documents*. Write the commentaries and reflections around the projects and documents available to the student. Assemble the final portfolio projects using the format directions given to the student in sections 3, 4, and 5. Ask a peer or mentor to review these materials before submitting them to the evaluating administrator. Make any necessary corrections or revisions.

4.0 **Required Awareness Projects:** The administrator must complete all required projects listed as 4.1, 4.2, 4.3, and 4.4. For each project complete a report with the following five components parts:

(A) Meet with your evaluator to discuss how best to gather data related to this project. Include the date of the meeting in your final report.

(B) Gather the data and provide a one-to-four page summary.

(C) Write a summary (up to one-page) of your personal reflections and insights *prior* to conferencing with the evaluating administrator.

(D) Confer with the evaluating administrator to obtain his/her insights and note the date of your meeting in your final report.

(E) Write a summary (up-to-one page) of your personal reflections and insights *following* your conference with your evaluating administrator.

4.1 **Project #1 (Yearly Record):** During the duration of the school year keep a journal (description of daily projects and personal insights) of the projects in which you engage while being evaluated. This should be done daily.

4.2 **Project #2 (Planning and Enabling People to do Their Jobs):** Develop an annual cycle of the administrator's responsibilities. Note in a calendar-like format what they are, if (and when) they are to be on a group agenda such as one for Building Leadership Team or the School Board and where on the calendar work direction must be given by the administrator to ensure completion of the responsibility.

4.3 **Project #3 (Pupil Management Operations):** Complete all of the administrative duties necessary to meet the needs of the students assigned to you. For example, if supervised by the administrator being evaluated, some of those duties could include: Follow up on truancies or questionable absences. Observe the action on discipline referrals. Observe calls and conferences with parents. Observe the administrative representative in I.E.P. conferences. Observe interaction with support agencies such as probation, social services, county court, Office of Civil Rights, juvenile officer, division of family services, etc., as appropriate.

Observe conferences with and in-service to staff as necessary to meet the needs of students. Other duties resulting from this role.

4.4 **Project #4 (Conflict Analysis and Resolution):** Attend no fewer than two meetings that are designed to resolve educational/philosophical /procedural conflict where the administrator is expected to assume the role of mediator. Compare and contrast the your behavior and style with other participants.

5.0 **Skill Building Projects:** the administrator must select ten projects from those listed below (5.1-5.20). For each of the ten projects complete a report with the **five** required component parts that follows:

(A)   Meet with your evaluating administrator to discuss how best to gather data related to this project. Include the date of the meeting in your final report.

(B)   Gather the data and provide a summary (one-to-four pages).

(C)   Write a summary (up to one-page) of your personal reflections and insights *prior* to conferencing with the evaluating administrator.

(D)   Confer with the evaluating administrator to obtain his/her insights and note the date of your meeting in your final report.

(E)   Write a summary (up-to-one page) of your personal reflections and insights *following* your conference with your evaluating administrator.

5.1   **Project #1 (Mail Review):** Read every piece of first class mail (electronic and hard copy) that comes to your office for a consecutive five-day period over two time spans. Each time span must be spaced by more than one week (ten days in all). Determine what mail should go to other administrators on a high priority or routine basis, what should be routed to others with a memo from you.

5.2   **Project #2 (Present Proposal):** Prepare and present a report or proposal to one of the following groups. The report must be done in writing as well as orally during a regular group meeting. Analyze what went well or not according to plan, and how you would change things if it all could be done over again. The administrative Council (a decision-making group at the building and or district level) or a PTA/PTO Council or comparable group such as finance advisory committee, site council, or district-wide committee.

5.3   **Project #3 (Lead a Meeting):** The administrator should conduct all or a portion of three separate meetings. Set forth in advance what you think should and will happen, analyze after the fact what you think did happen, and assess what changes, if any, you would make next time regarding advance preparation and delivery. Include the agendas and materials utilized in your presentations in the **portfolio** submitted to your evaluating administrator.

5.4   **Project #4 (Use of Technology):** (Part A) Identify "state-of-the art" use of technology for a school, that is, describe what an outside observer would expect to see in a school setting where technology has been given high priority status over a ten-year period. (Part B) Develop an evaluation tool or instrument that will help you determine the extent to which a given school measures up to the "state-of-the art" reference point. (Part C) Apply your instrument to the school where you are assigned as an administrator, analyze results, and formulate recommendations.

5.5*   **Project #5 (Budget):** Identify the factors/variables that must be considered in the building level budget process for the general and capital projects funds. Establish a time line for each process and identify whom to involve. Include the academics, activities, building projects, and general fund budgets. In addition, reflect on the unique challenges in administering and monitoring these two groupings: District allocation funds (general and capital projects), Building level activity funds (monies generated by clubs, or athletic groups and such thing as "picture money").

5.6*   **Project #6 (Staffing/Scheduling):** Work with the personnel director to establish the steps and time lines to determine the number of staff required for all aspects of the building level program and for developing a master schedule. What are the determining factors used to pair the number of staff desired to match the actual building allocation, enrollment and master schedule? If increases are projected, what steps will be taken to fill the positions? Consider balances and certification availability. If decreases are projected, what criteria will be used to make the cuts? What is the plan for maintaining morale during the downsizing?

5.7 **Project #7 (Instructional Styles):** Select a cross-section of five teachers at random from the teacher population of the building. Do a walk-through observation three (3) times within one class period for each teacher, noting the instructional strategy, which is being utilized at that time. Categorize the variety of instructional strategies observed according to learning styles addressed through each. Analyze the data and make recommendations addressing implementation strategies to ensure equity in educational opportunity. Document the teaching steps outlined in the **new Performance Based Teacher Evaluation model.**

5.8 **Project #8 (Personnel Selection):** Write a posting for a vacant licensed position. Develop an application form for the district. Participate in the screening of applicants. Identify the stakeholder groups who will be represented on the interview committee and write your reason(s) for including each of them. Propose a minimum of ten (10) interview questions. Also, identify subjects about which questions may not be asked. Prepare a rating scale for candidate comparison.

5.9* **Project #9 (Assessment):** Select one of the standardized assessments used in your school. Disaggregate the data and analyze the results. What natural groups sort out? What common characteristics define the groups? What generalizations about student achievement within the groups can be drawn and defended based on the data? What policy, procedure, and program adjustments would you recommend based on the data? How would you communicate the analysis results and the recommended policy, procedure, and program adjustments to your staff, the superintendent and other affected central office personnel, the school board, and your parent population? Develop a **school improvement plan** utilizing the data that you have identified.

5.10 **Project #10 (Vision):** List your personal and professional beliefs that you use as an administrator. Place a "one" by those statements you would NOT be willing to compromise, even if it means loss of promotion or loss of position. Place a "two" by those statements you WOULD be willing to compromise in order to achieve some other purpose deemed to be important. In addition, place an * by all statements you experienced during your career as an administrator.

5.11 **Project #11 (Physical Plant Health and Safety):** List no less than ten external health and safety issues that must be addressed on school property (for example, playground equipment, bus-loading, traffic patterns, signage). List a minimum of ten inside the school building health and safety issues (for example, blind spots for supervision, bathrooms, air quality, traffic patterns). From each list of ten select five (5) that theoretically need to be changed, identify the district personnel who need to be involved, and cite the procedures that must be followed to facilitate the change. Differentiate the processes used for emergency versus routine changes.

5.12 **Project #12 (Physical Plant Planning):** (Part A.) In the context of the school where you are assigned as an administrator, list the ten top items (roof, carpet, updating spaces) that must be included in a five-year plan for facility maintenance and improvements. (Part B.) Identify the resources that are made available for such purposes. (Part C.) Prioritize the projects. (Part D.) Identify the people that must be drawn upon for information to complete the five-year plan. (Part E.) Select a particular project and identify major factors (for example, personnel allocations, room assignments, exceptions to routines, cost over-runs and backup plans for projects that interfere with instructional time) that must be considered and planned to bring this project in on time, within budget and with minimal disruption.

5.13* **Project #13 (Conducting Performance Evaluation):** Identify district-established criteria by which performance based teacher evaluation will be conducted for a certificated employee. Gathers data regarding performance of a certificated employee(s) (for example, on-site observation). Using the data gathered, write your *official* performance based teacher evaluation report. Discuss this report with your evaluating administrator.

5.14 **Project #14 (Facilitating change):** Design a model (building level, multi-building, or district wide) to structure teamwork time for staff that facilitates ongoing curriculum planning, implementation of strategies, school improvement plan, or staff development. Analyze the contractual and internal political implication and considerations of your model.

5.15 **Project #15 (Clarifying Job Descriptions):** Determine what expectations a cross section of stakeholders* in the school district hold for a school administrator. Develop open-ended questions to be asked of all stakeholders. Obtain answers from all stakeholders by one or more of the following means: telephone interviews,

230

written surveys, or person interviews. At least three of the interviews must be done in person. Use the same open-ended questions in each case; map out those expectations, which are common to all stakeholder groups and those, which seem to be unique. Identify what you should and can do to meet these expectations. *Those interviewed must include the following: a school board member, a principal and a teacher at the elementary, middle, and high school level, PTO/PTA president, an employee union/professional organization president, a non-certificated employee such as a custodian, food service, or office employee, a person who owns and operates a business in the community, a citizen-at-large with no children in school, a middle school student, a high school student, a parent of an elementary student, a parent of a middle school student, and a parent of a senior high school student.

5.16*   Project #16 (Professionalism):   Join either the State Secondary School Principals, State Elementary School Principals, State Middle School Principals, Special Education Directors, or the Vocational Directors Association(s) (the administrator should become a member of the Regional Elementary and/or Secondary Principals Association). Study the services your organization provides and note how they may be accessed. Participate in at least two of the following: statewide and/or regional meetings, seminars or workshops sponsored by the association. Provide a summary of each.

5.17   Project #24 (Special Education):   Interview three parents of special education students. Choose parents of students with different handicapping conditions. What are the hopes each has for his/her child upon graduation or moving to the next level of education? What are the policies, procedures, and attitudes that the parent has found helpful in working with the school to meet the child's needs? What are the policies or attitudes the parent has encountered that have made it difficult for the parent and child to have a successful school experience? Based on these responses, write a set of goals and a plan of action for each goal that reinforces or changes current practices in dealing with special education students. Include a discussion of any ramifications your goals and plans would have for staffing, staff development, the budget, and space allocation in the physical plant, transportation, scheduling and public relations.

5.18 **Project # 18 (Activities):** Develop an annual cycle of student activities' programs at the school level. Include extra and co-curricular activities as well as school assemblies and "spirit" activities. Identify the policies and procedures that apply to each category of activities. Determine the budget and staffing considerations for each group of programs.

5.19 **Project #19 (Choice Project):** Carry out a proposal or project that will serve building purposes, do the legwork involved, and carry out an evaluation as appropriate. The above must prior approval by the evaluating administrator.

5.20 **Project #20 (Auxiliary Services):** Select one situation in which the administrator must work with an auxiliary provider and/or supervisor to resolve conflicts or implement related services. Some examples are food service, custodial, special education, police liaison, community education or transportation. Analyze the internal political implications and considerations of the situation and its resolution.

APPENDIX B

Form A

LOG OF PROJECTS

Name of Administrator: _____

Date: __/__/__

Name of Project: _____

Location of Project: _____

Description and value of Project:

_____   _____
Evaluating Administrator's Signature   Administrator's Signature

Phone # _____   Phone #_____

Form B

ADMINISTRATIVE AGREEMENT FORM

NAME OF ADMINISTRATOR: _____

EVALUATION TIME PERIOD: _____ YEAR _____

NAME OF EVALUATOR: _____

NAME OF ADMINISTRATOR'S SCHOOL: _____

Projects to be completed. These must have the approval of the evaluating supervisor and the administrator. Use this form to explore some tasks. The final plans will be established after the administrator receives the <u>Portfolio Policies- Procedure-projects manual.</u>

*Required	*Required	
4.1	5.5	Select 5 additional projects from
4.2	5.6	section 5.0
4.3	5.9	
4.4	5.13	
	5.16	

_____

*Signature of Evaluator   Phone Number

_____

Signature of Administrator   Phone Number

Completion of Portfolio:

Task Completed Satisfactorily?   ___Yes ___No   Date: _____

Log Completed Satisfactorily?   ___Yes ___No   Date: _____

Form C

PERSONAL INFORMATION:

Date: _____ / / _____

Name_____

My Present Position: _____

Home Address_____
_____

School Address   _____
                     _____

                Phone Number   Home ( ) _____
                                     School ( ) _____

Evaluating Adm.   _____

School Address   _____
_____
_____

References

AASA. (1993). <u>Making Sense of Testing & Assessment</u>. American Association of School Administrators. Library of Congress. 93-072247.

AASA. (1993). <u>Speaking & Writing Skills for Educators</u>. American Association of School Administrators. Library of Congress. 92-74902.

Ashbaugh & Kasten. (1991). <u>Educational Leadership</u>. Longman Publishing Group. White Plains, N.Y.

Brown, Irby, & Neumeyer. (1998). Taking the lead: one district's approach to principal evaluation. <u>NASSP Bulletin, 82,</u> 18-25

Durfour & Eaker. (1998). <u>Professional Learning Communities at Work: Best Practices For Enhancing Student Achievement</u>. National Educational Service. Bloomington, Indiana.

Ediger, Marlow. (1998). <u>Appraising the school principal.</u> Tests, measurement and evaluation clearinghouse. Missouri

Fischer, Schimmel, & Kelly. (1999). <u>Teachers And The Law</u>. Addison Wesley Longman, Inc. New York.

<u>Interstate School Leaders Licensure Consortium Standards for School Leaders,</u> (1996). Council of Chief State School Officers, Washington, D.C.

Lashway, Larry (1998,). Standards for administrators. <u>Research Roundup, 15,</u> n1.

Lashway, Larry (1998). Instruments for evaluation. <u>School Administrator, 55,</u> n9, 14-16 & 18-19

Murphy & Shipman. (1998, April). The interstate school leaders licensure consortium: A standards-based approach to strengthening educational leadership. Paper presented at the annual meeting of the American Educational Research Association, San Diego, CA.

NASSP Board of Directors. (March 1999). Statement of Ethics. NASSP Bulletin (p. 91).

Reeves, Douglas B. (1998), Holding Principals Accountable. School Administrator, 55, n9, 6-9

Sergiovanni, T. & Starratt, R. (1993). Supervision: A redefinition. New York: McGraw-Hill, Inc.

Shipman, Topps, & Murphy. (1998, April). Linking the ISLLC standards to professional development and relicensure. Paper presented at the annual meeting of the American Educational Research Association, San Diego, CA.

Wallace, Richard C. Jr. (1996). From Vision to Practice: The Art of Educational Leadership. Thousand Oaks, California: Corwin Press, Inc.

Wallace, Engel, & Mooney. (1997). The Learning School: A guide to Vision-Based Leadership. Thousand Oaks, California: Corwin Press, Inc.

Index

MELLEN STUDIES IN EDUCATION

18. Peter P. DeBoer, **Origins of Teacher Education at Calvin Colege, 1900-1930: And Gladly Teach**

19. Célestin Freinet, **Education Through Work: A Model for Child-Centered Learning**, John Sivell (trans.)

20. John Sivell (ed.), **Freinet Pedagogy: Theory and Practice**

21. John Klapper, **Foreign-Language Learning Through Immersion**

22. Maurice Whitehead, **The Academies of the Reverend Bartholomew Booth in Georgian England and Revolutionary America**

23. Margaret D. Tannenbaum, **Concepts and Issues in School Choice**

24. Rose M. Duhon-Sells and Emma T. Pitts, **An Interdisciplinary Approach to Multicultural Teaching and Learning**

25. Robert E. Ward, **An Encyclopedia of Irish Schools, 1500-1800**

26. David A. Brodie, **A Reference Manual for Human Performance Measurement in the Field of Physical Education and Sports Sciences**

27. Xiufeng Liu, **Mathematics and Science Curriculum Change in the People's Republic of China**

28. Judith Evans Longacre, **The History of Wilson College 1868 to 1970**

29. Thomas E. Jordan, **The First Decade of Life, Volume I: Birth to Age Five**

30. Thomas E. Jordan, **The First Decade of Life, Volume II: The Child From Five to Ten Years**

31. Mary I. Fuller and Anthony J. Rosie (eds.), **Teacher Education and School Partnerships**

32. James J. Van Patten (ed.), **Watersheds in Higher Education**

33. K. (Moti) Gokulsing and Cornel DaCosta (eds.), **Usable Knowledges as the Goal of University Education: Innovations in the Academic Enterprise Culture**

34. Georges Duquette (ed.), **Classroom Methods and Strategies for Teaching at the Secondary Level**

35. Linda A. Jackson and Michael Murray, **What Students Really Think of Professors: An Analysis of Classroom Evaluation Forms at an American University**

36. Donald H. Parkerson and Jo Ann Parkerson, **The Emergence of the Common School in the U.S. Countryside**

37. Neil R. Fenske, **A History of American Public High Schools, 1890-1990: Through the Eyes of Principals**

38. Gwendolyn M. Duhon Boudreaux (ed.), **An Interdisciplinary Approach to Issues and Practices in Teacher Education**

39. John Roach, **A Regional Study of Yorkshire Schools 1500-1820**